The
Smart Money Guide
to
Buying a Home

Ten Steps to Owning a Great Home
and a Great Investment

FLIP KENYON
&
HEATHER KENYON

The
Smart Money Guide
to
Buying a Home

Ten Steps to Owning a Great Home *and* a Great Investment

Manufactured in the United States of America
Library of Congress Catalog Card Number 98-092002
ISBN: 1-892786-00-1
Page Design: Sylvia Hemmerly, Publishing Professionals
Cover Design: Bob Denton, Denton, French & Daniel
Setup and Typography: Publishing Professionals
Printing Coordinator: Barbara Hagen
Editor: Rose M. Grant
Public Relations: Point to Point Communications
Contributing Editor: Stephanie Mayer

Publisher's Cataloging-in-Publication
(Provided by Quality Books, Inc.)

Kenyon, Flip.
     The smart money guide to buying a home : ten steps
to owning a great home and a great investment / Flip
Kenyon and Heather Kenyon. —1st ed.
     p. cm.
     Includes index.
     LCCN: 98-92002
     ISBN: 1-892786-00-1

     1. House buying—United States. 2. Mortgage
loans. 3. Real estate investment. 1. Kenyon,
Heather. II. Title.

HD1379.K46 1999   643'12
                                                       QBI98-1581

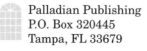 Palladian Publishing
P.O. Box 320445
Tampa, FL 33679

*This book is dedicated to our clients and
to home buyers everywhere. . .*

*Thanks to our friends and family
for their love and support*

Table of Contents

The Smart Money Guide to Buying a Home

About the Authors

Floyd J. "Flip" Kenyon graduated from Wake Forest University and worked in marketing and real estate in New York City and Tampa before starting his own firm, Kenyon Real Estate Appraisal & Investment, a Tampa-based real estate brokerage corporation. Presently, he is a licensed real estate broker and a state-certified residential real estate appraiser. Having signed over 10,000 appraisal reports, managed and closed hundreds of real estate investment deals, and represented many real estate buyers, he is an expert in the field of real estate valuation and investment.

Heather Warren Kenyon graduated from the University of Florida and traveled extensively throughout the United States, collecting vast experience in both local and national sales. Presently, she is a Realtor, Accredited Buyer Representative, licensed mortgage broker, and vice-president and director of the investment division of Kenyon Real Estate Appraisal and Investment. Specializing exclusively in real estate buyer representation for many years, she has helped hundreds of individuals find and purchase the home of their dreams.

To learn more about their company, visit their web site:

www.FloridaValue.com

or contact them at:

KENYON REAL ESTATE
Appraisal & Investment
P.O. Box 320445
Tampa, Florida 33679-2445

Phone: (813) 289-2200
Fax: (813) 289-2600
E-mail address: FJK5@msn.com

The Smart Money Guide to Buying a Home

Preface

After signing over 10,000 state-certified residential appraisal reports and helping hundreds of people purchase homes, we were sure of one thing: We are uniquely qualified to write a book about buying a home. But more than that, we felt it was important to answer the questions we hear daily and to offer a buyer's guide to choosing the right home at the right price with the highest investment potential.

The act of buying a home occurs more frequently in the average person's life now than ever before. According to a National Association of Realtors survey, "The Home Buying and Selling Process 1997," the average length of time a home is owned is only seven years. This means that buying a home with good resale potential is vital.

Purchasing real estate today is a complicated process and most people — not just first-time home buyers — are in danger of making major financial mistakes due to a lack of knowledge. Although the benefits of owning real estate outweigh the risks, the decision to buy a home is only the first of many choices you'll have to make along the path to home ownership. Regardless of the product, every purchase involves a series of choices, but buying a home may involve more choices than any other type of purchase. These choices may greatly impact your quality of life and financial status for years to come. In fact, your next home purchase may turn out to be the most complex and important purchase of your life.

Don't let that intimidate you. The most important and valuable tool the home buyer has is information. By arming yourself with enough information before you enter into the home buying process, you are increasing your chances of walking away with the keys to a smart investment. This book is devoted to helping you make the smartest choices when purchasing your home.

The order of the book is important, as it traces the specific order of the home buying process. Each chapter represents the right step in the order you'll need to take as you move toward home ownership. For example, it would make sense that setting a budget or considering what type of property to target should occur before house hunting.

Initially we detail the implications of real estate ownership and explain the mortgage game while helping you establish a budget based on typical lending guidelines. Next we'll emphasize the benefits of exclusive buyer representation, explore the types of residential real estate from which to choose and guide you through an efficient search for a home. This includes 20 ways to maximize investment potential when choosing your home and real life examples of how to and how not to buy a home. Finally we'll explain the real estate valuation process and how to make an offer with a shrewd sales contract, detail the inspection and closing process, offer a timeline of the move into your new home and suggest some smart money home improvements.

At the conclusion of each chapter is a section called "Things To Do," which summarizes the information discussed and makes specific suggestions for action. As a buyer, you can think about your individual situation, make notes on preferences and decide on your needs and constraints in preparation for each phase of your home purchase. We've also included The Ultimate Residential Real Estate Glossary of Terms and an appendix filled with the many forms and charts applicable to the purchasing process.

Due to the amount of money invested, the numerous service individuals involved, the risk of rip-off and the vast amount of legal paperwork, the purchase of a home should be seen not just as a way of meeting a need for shelter, but as a complex investment decision. Both first-time home buyers and seasoned professionals will benefit from this book. This informative guide is full of insider tips, offering a street-smart perspective to purchasing residential real estate that goes way beyond the basics.

The Ten Smart Money Steps to Buying a Home

There are ten steps to buying the right home at the right price with the best investment potential. Each chapter in this book represents one of these steps. Below is a summary of what you're about to read:

- Step (1) Consider the benefits, risks and commitment of a home purchase. Analyze your personal financial and tax situation. What can you afford and what do you need? Make the decision to buy now or wait until the time is right.

- Step (2) Shop loan sources, consider mortgage types, become pre-qualified for a loan and verify that you are financially ready to buy.

- Step (3) Hire a good real estate agent who specializes in buyer representation, discuss your housing needs, and understand how your agent can help you buy a home.

- Step (4) Decide on a lender, apply for loan and set a specific budget through the pre-approval process.

- Step (5) Consider how you would legally own your home, and decide on the location, design, and type of home you want.

- Step (6) Conduct routine, efficient searches for a home with your broker's guidance, consider real estate investment factors and select a home to buy.

- Step (7) Estimate the market value of the residence via a Comparative Market Analysis or state-certified residential real estate appraisal.

- Step (8) Prepare an offer using a contract for sale based on your estimate of value of the home, negotiate and execute the final contract, and have the home inspected.

- Step (9) Buy homeowner's insurance and provide the lender with other required items for final loan approval, review closing costs, perform the final walk-through of your home and attend the closing.

- Step (10) Move into your home and renovate over time, considering appropriate, smart money home improvement projects and methods for financing the work.

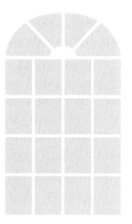

An Introduction to Home Ownership

Psychologists consider buying a home to be as stressful as divorce, serious illness, death and other life-changing events. But the more you know about buying a home, the less stressful the process becomes. Being aware of all options and potential pitfalls means you'll be able to make the right series of informed decisions in the right order and you may even enjoy doing so.

Your reasons for deciding to purchase real estate may include changing housing requirements, the desire to invest or own a vacation residence, or simply that you are ready to stop throwing rent money out the window. Whatever the reason, owning a home can offer many benefits. In fact, this purchase not only could improve your lifestyle, but it may turn out to be the best investment of your life.

Timing Is Everything: To Buy or Not to Buy

Timing is everything in real estate. There are many things to consider before you buy a home. You will incur the responsibility of mortgage payments and caring for a home. Your money will be tied up in an investment that is not necessarily considered liquid. The pros outweigh the cons, and potential pitfalls can be avoided by working with the best professionals. But everything

— good and bad — should be considered, as the timing of your purchase or the decision to buy could be affected.

First, think about all the reasons for making the purchase. Do you want to begin building wealth and stop wasting money in rent payments? Do you want a different lifestyle with a new housing arrangement? Do you want a vacation home? Are you looking for a way to diversify your investment portfolio with a safer, long-term investment? Do you need a tax write-off? All of these are good reasons for buying real estate.

Second, consider whether or not you are in a position to buy. If you are making an investment, is it a buyer's market or seller's market? If your current investment portfolio is presently made up of only stocks, bonds and mutual funds, do you need to diversify? If your job requires you to move a great deal, do you plan to remain in the area for a sufficient amount of time to warrant a purchase?

Given closing costs and the amount of time needed for a property to appreciate in value, it may not make sense for you to buy now if you do not plan to live in the home for more than three years. If you want a larger home, can you afford it, based on your current income and savings? Or is your current income actually so high that you need a good tax deduction? Do you have credit problems that may prevent you from securing a loan? Will your future income and housing requirements be changing and will the home be affordable and functional then?

It's easier to answer these questions when you consider in more detail the implications and benefits of owning real estate. Now may be a good time to meet with your accountant or financial planner. The process of applying for a loan or becoming prequalified at a bank will also help you answer questions regarding the affordability of a home.

Many people try to time their purchase according to market conditions. Obviously, buying during a down market, or a "buyer's market" is best, but just when is this? Estimating what the market will do in the future — especially the real estate market — is virtually impossible. A down market is usually short-lived anyway, so if you're ready to buy, do it now. We believe you should buy when it's best for your personal situation.

We're not saying to disregard present market conditions, as this may affect the amount you offer. In a buyer's market, you can usually get away with low-ball offers. Conversely, in a seller's market, homes are frequently purchased at full list price, so offers need to be higher. Market conditions should not affect your decision to buy or the timing of your purchase.

Like any investment — or long term relationship — a smart real estate purchase involves commitment. Your decision to buy should be partially based on your level of devotion to the purchasing process. Buying a home takes hard work, time, research and reliance on many real estate professionals. Finding a home involves more than just driving the streets and searching for a property that appeals to you. You must set a budget and apply for a loan. You must be familiar with the market, the real estate valuation process, the types of properties and mortgages from which to choose and what to look for when shopping for a home.

Sales agents, attorneys, inspectors and appraisers must be hired. These individuals may not be looking out for your best interests, so choosing the right ones will take time. Negotiating, contracting, inspecting and closing on a property can take even more time. The entire process of purchasing a home, from the time you begin actively searching until closing, can take as little as one month or as long as six months or more. This largely depends on your needs, buying experience, financial status, level of participation and the inventory and availability of properties in the marketplace.

Once the decision is made to buy, be prepared to devote yourself 100 percent to the purchasing process. Make the time to do it right. Allocate certain hours each day to investigate and work with service individuals, inspect properties or meet with lenders. Choose a time of year that makes the most sense for this effort. Make sure to plan ahead and enlist the help of family and friends if necessary.

Tax Advantages:
Uncle Sam Lends a Hand

Home ownership is becoming more and more profitable, thanks to many of the new tax laws that encourage home buying. The tax benefits associated with owning residential real estate are superior to most other investments. Homeowners can claim basic items as deductible, such as property taxes and mortgage interest charges. Deductions for home mortgage interest can apply to first or second homes. Rental properties also qualify for depreciation allowances as a tax benefit.

Tax laws are frequently changing and your personal tax situation may be unique. It is important to consult a tax advisor before purchasing so you stay current and know how real estate ownership affects your personal tax return.

Some of today's real estate tax codes have been in effect for a while. Specifically, interest paid on mortgage loans of up to 1 million dollars that is used to buy, build or substantially improve your property is fully deductible. Presently the mortgage limit is $500,000 for married couples filing separately. Interest on home equity loans is deductible for loans up to $100,000, and $50,000 for married persons filing separately.

Points are also allowed as itemized deductions. A point is equal to a percentage of the loan amount. The borrower is sometimes charged points by the lender. Points may be part of the up-front costs you are required to pay in order to get a mortgage loan. The government considers points as pre-paid interest, because they are payment for the use of money. It is important to remember that points can be deducted the year they are paid. If you borrow to pay these points, you can also deduct the resulting interest payments as part of your first mortgage deduction.

Another big advantage of home ownership, a "rollover benefit," occurs when you sell your property. The tax on the profit of a sale of a primary residence can be deferred completely if you buy or build another house and meet a *principal test* and a *time test*.

✔ The *principal test* requires you to show that you have used your old home as your primary, or principal, residence and that you will use your new home as a principal residence.

✔ The *time test* requires that you live in a residence two of the last five years for it to be considered your primary residence.

A couple now can gain up to $500,000 and an individual can gain up to $250,000 in profits from the sale of a home tax-free. If you lose money on the sale of your home, you can't deduct that loss from your taxes.

There are also tax breaks for home buyers who are having difficulty coming up with enough money for a down-payment on their first home. The government is allowing first-time home buyers to use their Individual Retirement Accounts to make initial down payments without paying a tax penalty. Gifts can be accepted to buy a house from the IRAs of parents or grandparents under the age of 59 with no penalty. Income tax must still be paid on any amount withdrawn.

> *A couple now can gain up to $500,000 and an individual can gain up to $250,000 in profits from the sale of a home tax-free*

In a few states, homestead laws are also in place which protect a family's primary home, or homestead, from being seized by creditors, assuming your mortgage payments have been paid. Homesteads can also qualify for a partial exemption from property taxes. In Florida, for example, homeowners are allowed to deduct $25,000 from the assessed value of their primary residence. Since the property tax on a home is based on its assessed value, the effective tax paid on a homestead is reduced. This exemption may not be automatic and an application may have to be filed with your local government's property appraiser's office.

Because tax laws are frequently changing, and everyone's situation is different, discover what deductions you qualify for by hiring a good tax professional.

Building Wealth: Securing Your Financial Future with Real Estate

Owning real estate is a great way to build wealth. Wealth, or *net worth*, is basically the difference between your debts and assets. Building wealth over time in a systematic, relatively low-risk fashion is the secret of most successful investors. This is exactly what real estate can offer you, if you purchase carefully. In fact, we believe real estate is the best investment you can make. Given the tax benefits, low risk, and potential for high returns and capital appreciation, real estate is better than stocks, bonds, risky business ventures – anything. Plus, it's the only investment that provides a place for you to live.

Building *equity* in a property, or the difference between a property's market value and what you owe on the mortgage, is one way you can build wealth as an owner of real estate. By simply making payments on time on your loan, you are reducing the principal, or loan amount of your mortgage. The gradual paying down of the mortgage is also known as *amortization* of the mortgage.

Building equity, even with the typical three to ten percent appreciation rates of real estate, can cause your money to grow faster than any investment. Historically this can't be debated. Unlike stock market investments, these gains grow free of local, state or federal income tax. Stock market pre-tax returns over the last century have averaged nine percent to twelve percent, depending on your information source. An after-tax stock return of ten percent is considered respectable if you look at a 30-year period, which is similar to the length of many mortgages. See Table 1.1, which shows how a yearly after-tax return of about 28 percent can be expected with only a 4 percent property appreciation.

Table 1.1
How only 4 percent appreciation in property value
can more than quadruple your original investment in 6 years:*

Year 1		Year 6	
Purchase price	$200,000	Market Value	$253,064
Mortgage	$180,000	Mortgage Balance	$167,381
Cash Invested	$ 20,000	Cash Equity	$ 85,683

*Assuming an interest rate of 7.25 percent on a fixed 30-year term loan.

The amount that goes toward reducing the principal is small at first, because you are paying interest on a larger loan amount. But remember that this larger interest portion also means a larger tax deduction. Later, in your retirement years, the need for a deduction from mortgage interest will decrease. Theoretically, by the time the interest portion is low or gone altogether, your income will also be lower, so from a tax perspective, it all works out well.

Because real estate usually appreciates in value over time, the gap between what you owe and what the property is worth widens and increases your net worth. As a general rule, real estate's ability to go up in value can make its purchase worthwhile usually after only a few years. In other words, this increase in equity due to an increase in property value will cover all expenses like closing costs, interest, insurance, and taxes associated with property ownership.

The ability to leverage money, or make loans against the equity in the property, is another financial benefit of owning real estate. Many investors buy one property after another, using properties already owned as collateral. Others use real estate as collateral for any type of loan, like home equity programs or second mortgages. This may finance education, business start-ups or other types of investments that could build wealth.

Rental income is another way to build wealth. Many investors build a portfolio of rental properties so large that they live off rent payments exclusively. The greater the positive cash flow from rent, the greater the income.

Renting while on vacation is like throwing money out the window, but many people still rent because they are not willing to make the commitment of additional home ownership or have not been able to save enough for the payments.

Owning a rental property or a vacation home that can be rented out to short-term tenants during the off season may be a solution. Instead of renting while on a vacation, many people are opting to own a vacation or second home due to the tax advantages and investment potential of owning real estate. Wealthy people do not own second homes only because they can afford to do so; they also own second homes for tax write-offs or for long-term investments. Many wealthy individuals intentionally maintain mortgages strictly for the tax deduction, even though financing the deal is unnecessary.

Mortgage interest and property taxes are also tax-deductible on a second home. Vacation homes, especially those on the water or on a golf course, will most likely appreciate in value. In Florida, vacation homes are an extremely popular way for many to invest and maintain a get-away shelter. Businesses that own vacation homes for the enjoyment of their associates and clients deduct costs as a business expense.

Some buy residences strictly to rent to long- or short-term tenants. Rental payments help pay off the mortgage while the property appreciates in value, thus building equity. At the same time, landlords may enjoy a positive rental income. Rental properties also qualify for depreciation allowances as a tax benefit.

If you want the benefits of both a second home and a rental property, you can buy a multi-unit apartment and live rent-free in one of the units while the tenants pay the mortgage. In this way, one can act as an on-site owner landlord. Some individuals rent out to tenants for part of the year while remaining up north, then fly south to live in the residence for the other part of the year.

An arrangement offering similar benefits is a time-share, where several individuals retain part-ownership interest in one residence and take turns actually residing in the home. This reduces an individual's risk, commitment and investment, while offering use of a great part-time vacation home.

Things to Do

☐ Educate yourself. Read this and other books cover to cover. With knowledge and the right real estate professionals working for you, stress will be reduced and your enjoyment of the process will increase.

☐ Consider your reasons for buying a home, the purpose it will serve and the specific benefits you will receive. What are the potential pitfalls?

☐ Decide whether you are ready to make the financial and time commitment necessary to make the purchase. Timing is important, so plan ahead.

☐ Check out interest rates and the real estate market in general.

☐ Review your personal finances. Meet with your tax advisor or financial planner to review the financial implications associated with buying various types of properties.

☐ Discuss the purchase with any family member who will be affected by the purchase.

☐ Get serious about buying a home and plan when the effort should begin. Once the decision is made, you have to be prepared to attack the effort full force in order to purchase the best property for the best price with the best investment potential.

Step 2

Financing Options

The first step to home ownership is to examine your financing options by shopping for loan sources and considering various mortgage types for the loan associated with your purchase. You can then select a specific lender and become pre-qualified for a certain loan amount. Here, we will detail loan source options such as banks and mortgage brokers, and review various types of mortgages available to today's buyer.

Loan Sources:
Because Money Doesn't Grow on Trees

Today, there are many loan sources from which to choose. Shopping for a loan by visiting more than one lender or mortgage broker is a good idea. Like anything else, comparison-shopping and referrals may lead you in the right direction. Ask your real estate broker, friends or family to suggest some companies they have used in the past.

Generally national banks offer many mortgage options and services and may have competitive rates, but may also be stricter with their lending guidelines. Credit unions and local or regional banks may be more flexible in underwriting loans, but may not offer the range of services that a national bank can. For example, on-line banking, where you perform banking functions on your computer, is a great service many banks now offer.

11

You may already be familiar with a certain bank and its loan officers. Applying for a loan at a bank where you already have an account can be more convenient, especially if your financial profile is solid. They will be more familiar with you and your accounts, and the application process may be easier.

Using a mortgage broker is a good option because they can connect to many different lenders and loan programs. Their role is to act as a middleman between a lender and a borrower. Frequently, first-time home buyers will have better success with a mortgage broker because they will be able to choose between many loan programs to find the best one. Less-than-perfect financial profiles may mean higher interest rates or other charges, but the chances of securing a loan may be better. Real estate or mortgage brokerage offices have Computer Loan Origination systems that help sort through the various types of loans offered by different lenders. The CLO operator may charge a fee for the service, and the buyer or the selected lender may pay the fee.

The lender, the borrower or both may pay the mortgage broker. Comparing the fees that mortgage brokers charge for their services can save you thousands of dollars in the long run. A good way to do this is to compare the Annual Percentage Rate (APR) from lender to lender. The APR includes the interest rate, points, mortgage broker fees and other fees you may have to pay. Points are usually paid to the lender, mortgage broker or both, at the settlement or completion of escrow. The Truth in Lending Act (Consumer Protection Act), also known as Regulation Z, requires lenders to show the borrower what the APR is and detail other payment information associated with the loan.

Mortgage banks or mortgage companies now generate the majority of mortgage loans. Unlike traditional banks, they do not offer savings or checking accounts. These are banks that specialize in mortgages, packaging and selling them in the secondary market to investors. These investors can be life insurance companies, commercial banks, savings and loan associations, mutual savings banks, or pension, trust or retirement funds. Institutional lenders are often in the position of a mortgage banker. In some cases, they will sell the loans to other investors, usually in the secondary market, and then service the loans for the investors. In compensation, they receive a fee based on the principal balance of the loan each year from mortgage buyer-investors.

Types of Mortgages: Which One is Best for You?

Today, there are more types of mortgages available than ever before. We will detail only the most common types of mortgages, but there are many others that may work for you. Each year, lenders who want to make loans more attractive are inventing new and creative mortgage programs. With names like graduated payment mortgage, shared appreciation mortgage, reduction option mortgage, price level adjusted mortgage, package mortgage, or reverse annuity mortgage, the mortgage game can be complex and confusing.

Deciding which mortgage is right for you has a lot to do with predicting where you may be financially in the future. For example, some mortgages have payments that balloon or increase in size as time goes on. Being able to handle this future financial burden and hoping that your income will continue to increase can be a stressful way to live. Yet it can also be a way to afford a home now when your income may be at a lower level.

Community Home Loan Programs are now also offered. They are ideal for first-time home buyers and can offer more flexible guidelines with smaller down payments. Usually associated with a county or state program, specific terms vary from area to area. The government is now making it easier for a first-time home buyer to purchase, so ask your local mortgage professional about these types of programs in your area.

Fixed Rate vs. Adjustable Rate Mortgages

Payment amounts and interest rates are fixed, or unchanging, with a fixed rate mortgage. Yet there are options regarding the term of the loan. Although 15- and 30-year terms are the most common, 5-, 10- and 25-year terms are also offered. Shorter term loans are becoming more popular, as borrowers are realizing how much less they would be paying over the course of the loan in total interest by choosing these types of mortgages.

Given a loan amount of $150,000 at a 7.5 percent interest rate, Table 2.1 shows the total dollar amounts for various loan terms:

Table 2.1 Loan Term Comparison

Loan Term	10 years	15 years	30 years
Monthly Payment	$ 1,781	$ 1,391	$ 1,049
Total Paid by End of Term	$213,664	$250,294	$377,575
Total Interest Paid	$ 63,663	$100,293	$227,576

(See Appendix for a sample Amortization Schedules showing monthly interest charges for 10-, 15- and 30-year loans.)

The borrower can have the option of paying off the loan before the end of the term without penalty. This effectively reduces the term and the amount of interest paid. Sometimes a prepayment penalty is charged, or the lender may not allow prepayment at all. Make sure prepayment is allowed. Many smart buyers choose a 30-year term because the monthly payments are lower, then pay off the loan early as extra money becomes available.

Lower rates can be expected if points are paid up front. One point is equal to one percent of the total mortgage. The borrower will also receive lower rates for shorter terms, but the payments will be higher because the borrower is paying the loan back in less time. If you are planning to be in your home for a long time, a fixed rate mortgage may be the best bet because the mortgage payment will not be changed for the length of the loan.

The higher the interest rate, the more interest that is paid. Over a 30-year period, this can really add up. The difference between a 6.5 percent loan and a 10.5 percent is enormous when considering the total amount paid.

Given a loan amount of $150,000 for 30 years, Table 2.2 shows the total dollar amounts for various interest rates:

Table 2.2 Loan Interest Rate Comparison

Annual Interest Rate	6.5%	7.5%	8.5%	9.5%	10.5%
Monthly Payment	$ 948	$ 1,049	$ 1,153	$ 1,261	$ 1,372
Total Paid in 30 Yrs.	$341,316	$377,575	$415,213	$454,061	$493,960
Total Interest Paid in 30 Yrs.	$191,317	$227,576	$265,213	$304,061	$343,959

Adjustable Rate Mortgages, or *ARMs*, are variable rate loans that have indexes or margins that determine how and when the interest and payment amounts change. The adjustment frequency period (which is the amount of time between rate changes) will vary depending on the lender. Your payment amount may change every year or six months. The one-year ARM may buy the most home because its initial rates and monthly payments are the lowest. However, with ARMs the buyer is subject to the ups and downs of interest rates.

When choosing an ARM, the buyer is betting on interest rates staying low. Usually there is a limit to the amount of change per year or over the length of the term. This limit is called a *cap* and is typically about 2 percent per year. The term *ceiling*, or *lifetime cap*, refers to the maximum amount an adjustable mortgage rate may rise over the life of the loan. This is usually about 5 percent.

There are also mortgages, such as the *Convertible ARM*, which permit borrowers to switch from an adjustable rate to a fixed one. There may be costs associated with the convertible classification, such as conversion fees or complex interest rate formulas, so be aware of all charges before committing to this type of loan.

FHA, VA and Assumable Mortgages

The Federal Housing Administration (FHA) was created in 1934 by the federal government. Today it is part of the Department of Housing and Urban Development (HUD) and acts as a mortgage insurance agency. The FHA protects lenders from the losses that occur when borrowers do not repay their loans. Lenders submit applications from borrowers to the local FHA office for approval. In many cases, FHA underwriting standards are a lot more lenient than conventional loan standards.

With an FHA loan you can use less money for a down payment and have a higher monthly debt allowance. Specifically, a borrower can put down as little as three to five percent and can have an income-to-debt ratio of up to 41 percent. (See Chapter 4 for an explanation of how an income-to-debt ratio is calculated.) Once the FHA has approved the loan application, it will then insure the lender for any losses that may result from default and foreclosure. However, borrowers are limited to the amount of money they can borrow, and the borrower remains liable to the federal government for any amount paid by the FHA to the lender. FHA will insure 30-year fixed, 15-year fixed and one-year adjustable programs. Contact your local HUD office or a mortgage broker for more details.

There are also loans insured by the Department of Veteran Affairs (or VA, as it is commonly called), which you may be eligible for. Although the VA can make loans, most loans are made by institutional lenders and are guaranteed by the VA to protect lenders if the veteran defaults. There are restrictions to this type of loan. For example, only veterans can apply, it must be a first mortgage and the owner must occupy the residence. If you are a veteran, this type of loan is great. No down payment is required and those with income-to-debt ratios of up to 41 percent can qualify. The VA will guarantee 30-year fixed, 15-year fixed, and one-year adjustable loan programs.

An assumable mortgage is one that stays with the property once it is sold. There are several benefits associated with the assumption of a mortgage. For example, a buyer can save on a number of costs associated with obtaining a new mortgage. Another advantage is that the house does not have to pass any evaluation by a lender. An assumable mortgage also prevents the interest rate of the loan from changing, and substantially speeds up the closing process.

FHA loans made before December 1, 1986 and VA loans made before March 1, 1998 are examples of assumable loans. Newer FHA and VA loans are assumable with bank approval. This means your income and credit must qualify through the lending institution. In any case, your credit and finances have to be in good shape before a seller would consider this type of arrangement, as the seller retains liability for the debt if the buyer fails to make the mortgage payments.

An assumable mortgage may be neither a selling point for the property nor a benefit to the buyer if the existing interest rate on the mortgage is much higher than present competitive rates. On the other hand, if the loan is assumable without bank approval, and your financial profile is not up to bank standards, this may be a way for you to buy a home.

Borrower Beware: Mortgage Pitfalls

It is important to realize that a mortgage broker can operate as an independent business and may not be looking out for your best interests. Therefore, it is crucial that you shop around for your loan and understand everything you are signing. This is particularly true for a first-time home buyer.

There are many ethical and trustworthy mortgage brokers and lenders who will be happy to explain any charges, fees, or papers they are asking you to sign. If the mortgage broker or lender is too vague or if the rate they are charging is high, you should ask questions until you're satisfied. If you have doubts about a lender or mortgage broker, you can call your state banking department to ask if the lender or broker is registered or licensed, and how long they have been in business. The banking department can also let you know if a lender has any consumer complaints on file.

With adjustable rate mortgages, be wary of lenders offering introductory interest rates. These are temporary, lower starting rates that can mask the ultimate rates to be charged. Because these introductory rates hide the true cost of the loan, it is hard to compare lenders. This practice also may call for the interest rate to adjust to the maximum amount each period until the note rate equals the index plus margin rate, no matter if the interest rate rises, falls, or remains stable. In other words, the interest rate is adjusted even though there is no rate index change. Make sure you understand the difference between the introductory rate and the note rate when considering this type of loan.

You should ask if a prepayment penalty is charged for paying off the loan before it is due. Ask about any costs that may be charged to you. Small costs can add up and no cost is necessarily standard or absolutely set in stone. Above all, negotiate. Remember that lenders are in business to make money. Charges such as points, application fees, or clauses that benefit the lender, such as prepayment penalties, can be avoided and negotiated down.

Things to Do

☐ Shop around for lenders and mortgage brokers.

☐ Investigate the various types of mortgages that are offered. When shopping around, it's important to carefully read and understand everything before you sign it and to ask plenty of questions. If the lenders or mortgage brokers are doing their job, they'll take the time to answer all of your questions so that you feel comfortable.

☐ Once certain lenders are specified, become pre-qualified for a loan. This not only helps to determine whether or not you can afford to buy, but it also gives you an estimated budget and a head start in the formal application process.

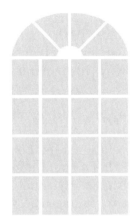

Step 3

Buyer Representation

We hope you've decided to hire a real estate agent to help you buy a home. This chapter will explain real estate agency relationships and terminology, the reasons why you should hire a buyer's broker, what to look for and what to expect when hiring one.

Are You Ready for a New Relationship ...With Your Agent?

Real estate agency relationships can be difficult to understand. How your agent or Realtor represents you in the real estate transaction is the important issue. Is your agent looking out for your best interests exclusively, or is he or she really representing the seller? Every state has slightly different agency laws, so have your agent explain how he or she is working for you.

Let's start with a definition of commonly used terms. A real estate agent (or broker) or *single agent* is someone who is authorized to act on behalf of another in dealing with third parties. In other words, that agent represents one party exclusively, whether it is the seller or the buyer. That agent is bound by certain *fiduciary duties*, to be discussed in detail later. A *Realtor* is associated with a broker who is a member of the National Association of Realtors.

In many states a *transaction broker* handles all aspects of the transaction, but can't divulge any confidential information to

21

either party and can represent both parties only in a limited form. With *dual agency*, the real estate broker represents both parties in a transaction from start to finish. We will explain later why this is not a good idea.

A *client (or principal)* is the party who hires a real estate agent. The agent represents this person's best interests at all times. A *customer (or prospect)* is a third party to the agency relationship. For example, the buyer is the customer of the seller's agent and the seller is the customer of the buyer's agent. This party is not the same as the client. A *subagent (or salesperson)* is one who works with another agent and is authorized to act on behalf of an agent (or broker) by the principal. (More definitions of commonly used real estate terms are included in the glossary section of this book.)

In 1983, a Federal Trade Commission study revealed that over 72 percent of all home buyers nationwide mistakenly believed they were being represented by the agent who was showing them homes. In fact, many buyers were sold homes by the agent protecting the seller's best interests. This practice continues in many states, but because of this finding by the FTC and a few lawsuits, real estate agency laws have started to change across the United States.

Depending upon the state in which you live, you can be represented in a number of ways. Dual agency, where the agent represents both sides of the transaction, is a type of representation that could be dying a quick death. Now the trend is to require that either the buyer or seller is represented, but not both. This makes sense, when you realize that a buyer and seller have opposing interests in a transaction. How can an agent fight for both parties' best interests at the same time? According to the law, attorneys can't do this, and soon, neither will a real estate agent. These new agency laws are protecting the buyer more and more.

In many states, acting as a transaction broker is one of the ways real estate agents can represent both sides of the transaction. Here, a limited form of representation is performed and an agent works only to facilitate the transaction. This means that a buyer or seller is not responsible for the acts of the agent, and both parties give up their rights to the undivided loyalty of the agent.

A transaction brokerage would occur if an agent brings a buyer/client to his own listing or was trying to sell a home to a buyer/client that was listed by his own company. In order to make sure that the seller and buyer have equitable representation, an agent would become a transaction broker. Have your agent explain these relationships and how they affect you in the state where you are purchasing real estate.

Exclusive Buyer Representation: Protecting Your Best Interests

Real estate professionals now must begin to choose who to represent. Although buyer representation is becoming a more popular and important specialization, seller representation may be less vital in the future. Or, at least, a seller will need to rely on a broker in a more limited role, as with a transaction broker.

Through the Internet and other marketing tools, sellers can get the word out about their property in more effective ways. In fact, the Internet may become the Multiple Listing Service of the future. Guided video tours of listings are now available on the Internet, complete with views of surrounding neighborhoods.

With these new innovations and knowledge of a home's market value, having an expert sell your home is less important than having an expert help you buy a home. Selling requires an ability to market and expose a product, with technology now doing much of the work. Selling real estate is similar to selling any other product. With familiarity of the product, exposure and a fair sales price, the product should sell. In the future, an appraiser may be more important than a sales agent to a seller. For now, we still recommend a seller use a broker to sell their home. However, with the speed at which technology and agency rules are changing, the way we buy and sell real estate will not stay the same for long.

Wide-ranging real estate knowledge is vital when buying a home. Enlisting the help of an expert, especially one required to fight for your best interests, is indispensable in finding and purchasing the right property at the right price. Hiring an agent who specializes in buyer representation, who is expert in real estate research, valuation, finance, and analyzing listing information is especially important. This kind of specialization is becoming more and more popular due to the ever-increasing complexity of the transaction and the way we search for a home.

Companies that represent only buyers specialize in what is called *exclusive buyer representation*. These companies never accept listings, so there is never a conflict of interest. There is never a temptation to push their own company's listings because they have none. Their agents act as real estate experts and consultants, not as salespeople. They do not care which property you buy, as long as it is the best property for you at the lowest price possible. Never buy a home from the seller's agent or an agent that normally represents sellers.

According to the April 1993 issue of *Money* magazine, U.S. Sprint (the long distance company) found that 232 relocating Sprint employees who hired buyer's brokers paid an average of 91 percent of a home's list price. People using traditional agents typically paid about 96 percent. On a house originally priced at $150,000, that's a difference of $7,500.

Agents who specialize in exclusive buyer representation sometimes earn an Accredited Buyer Representative designation. Offered by the Real Estate Buyer's Agent Council, Inc. of the National Association of Realtors, agents are required to take coursework in the specialization and represent a minimum number of buyers to earn the designation. The National Association of Exclusive Buyer Agents is another similar organization.

Choosing the Right Real Estate Agent

You should make sure your agent specializes in buyer representation and that he or she is representing only you in the transaction. Be careful — only a small percentage of all real estate agents exclusively represent buyers. A good agent is competent, knowledgeable, well educated and service-minded. Look for those with at least a four-year college degree and at least five years' experience working full-time in real estate. They should also be able to suggest sources of financing, prepare contracts, negotiate a low price and favorable terms, arrange for home inspections and be able to refer you to other qualified service individuals. Essentially their job is to make your life easier and put you in touch with qualified and trustworthy individuals who will represent your best interests.

Experience in real estate appraisal is important. You will be making a large investment in time and money when you buy a home and you want to make sure that you will eventually make money on the resale of that home. If your real estate agent is not informed about how homes are valuated, he or she could be losing you thousands of dollars by showing you properties that are overpriced or may not go up in value at a competitive rate. Of course, ask for references and a company brochure.

Here are a few questions to ask a real estate professional to test his/her level of knowledge and experience in buyer representation:

- ✔ What percentage of your company's business is representing buyers?
- ✔ Does your company accept listings or practice dual agency?
- ✔ What training in buyer representation have you had and do you hold any professional designations specific to buyer representation?
- ✔ How long have you been representing buyers?
- ✔ What are the benefits of working with a real estate agent who is an exclusive buyer representative?
- ✔ What forms am I required to sign and what do they mean?
- ✔ What are the fiduciary duties a real estate agent has when representing me and how might these duties be altered depending on the service role the agent has?

✔ What are the basic terms of a real estate contract and what clauses can you incorporate in our offer to protect me as a buyer?

✔ How is a real estate agent obligated to protect my financial interests and how can you help me save money?

✔ What is the purpose of the home inspection and how should I attempt to re-negotiate the terms if there are serious problems with the property?

✔ Can you provide me with a list of lenders, inspectors, attorneys, appraisers or insurance agents?

✔ What is the role of the lender and the appraiser in my home purchase, whose side are they on, and how do I know if the fees they charge are reasonable?

✔ What is the role of the title company in this transaction?

✔ What information about my buying needs should I be careful about disclosing or not disclosing to an agent working as a single agent or a transaction broker?

These are important items your real estate agent should be able to answer. Often just having the real estate agent explain the sales contract to you is enough to tell if an agent knows what he or she is talking about. Make sure that you are also comfortable with the agent. You will be spending a lot of time with this person, so make sure you feel at ease expressing what you want and need in a home.

One last word of caution, even though real estate agents represent you, they also are not paid until you find a home to buy. Don't feel pressured into making an offer on a house you're not sure of. However, if you find a great house in a good neighborhood that you like, don't hesitate! Good homes which are priced right do not stay on the market long.

Your Agent's Responsibilities: What Have You Done for Me Lately?

Once you choose an agent, he'll probably ask you to sign an agreement to guarantee that you'll work exclusively with him for a certain period of time. This contract will specify how the agent

Here are the fiduciary duties by which your agent is bound when operating as a *single agent*:

1. Dealing honestly and fairly. This should be an obvious part of doing business, but unfortunately, some agents need reminding.

2. Loyalty. Agents owe complete loyalty to the principal (client). A buyer's agent is obligated to protect the buyer's best interests, including fighting for the lowest purchase price possible. A seller's agent is loyal to the seller. Therefore, the buyer should not, under any circumstances, divulge any confidential information to the seller's agent.

3. Obedience. The agent is obligated to be obedient in regard to the buyer's or seller's instructions unless these instructions are against the law. An example of this would be a prospective home buyer instructing the agent not to show him any homes that are owned by a minority group. This is illegal and the agent can't obey this request.

4. Confidentiality. The confidentiality provision prevents the agent from disclosing that the buyer will pay a price greater than the price presented in a written offer, or that a seller will accept less than the offering price. The agent also can't divulge the motivation of the buyer for buying the property, that the buyer will agree to financing terms other than those offered, or any other information that the buyer wants to keep confidential. An exception to this would be if the buyers asked the agent to conceal that they were financially unable to buy the home. This could happen if the buyers had a home they had to sell before they could afford to buy a new home. The agent could not keep this from the seller's agent and the seller.

5. Full disclosure. The agent must fully disclose all known facts affecting the value of real property which aren't readily observable to the buyer. The seller's agent should provide the buyer with a disclosure form signed by the seller but if this isn't done, the buyer or buyer's agent should ask the seller's agent about any defects the seller may be aware of. The seller and the seller's agent are obligated to divulge this information.

6. Accounting for all funds. Any money, deeds, papers, documents or other items belonging to others and entrusted to an agent must be safeguarded and accounted for.

7. Skill, care and diligence. This refers to the agent's performance mainly during the transaction.

8. Presenting all offers in a timely manner. The agent is obligated to do this unless a party has previously directed the agent otherwise in writing.

is to be paid and details the agent's and the buyer's obligations. (See appendix for sample Exclusive Buyer Broker Agreement)

You may also be asked to sign disclosure forms, which tell you how you'll be represented in the transaction. If the agent does not provide you with an explanation of how you are being represented, make sure you ask. This is important because if the broker is representing the seller, you should be careful what you disclose. Don't tell that agent anything you would not want the sellers to know because the agent is legally obligated to divulge any information he knows to the sellers. If you are represented by a buyer's agent, that agent is bound by a fiduciary duty to look out for your best interests above everyone else's, including his own.

Therefore, when you enlist the help of a buyer's agent, your best interests will always be represented. Your bargaining position will be protected, because anything you say will remain confidential. Even your identity can remain anonymous. A buyer's agent will be very motivated to help you, especially if she knows you are working exclusively with her and will remain loyal. Remember that a real estate agent usually does not get paid unless you purchase a home, so it is in her best interest to keep you happy. A buyer's agent can save you time, money and effort.

The best part is that an agent acting as a buyer's representative traditionally receives payment from the seller through the proceeds of the sale. A buyer's agent may also be paid by the buyer on an hourly basis, on retainer, or on commission shared or split with the seller. Some buyer representatives may require a deposit from you that can eventually go towards the down payment on a property you choose to buy. However, these methods are not very common, and you can usually expect the seller to foot the bill for the services of your buyer's agent.

How Your Agent Can Help You Purchase a Home

In a way, the purchase of a home occurs in two phases — the search and the transaction. Your agent can help you in many ways throughout this process.

The search involves not only looking for homes but also the ability to access market information on all currently listed homes for sale, narrowing down properties that meet your needs and taking the time to routinely research and view these properties. Access to all current listing information is important, because new listings appear daily and good deals go fast. A home search also involves knowing the market and the neighborhoods. Your real estate agent can help you find a home more efficiently than if you were randomly driving the streets looking for properties or looking in a newspaper.

Finding the perfect home results from being aware of opportunities. As experts in real estate research, agents are aware of all homes actively listed for sale in the Multiple Listing Service and can show you any one of them. New construction, vacant lots, foreclosures and properties offered for sale by owner can also be analyzed and brought to your attention. Since new homes are listed daily, there is a big chance of missing out on new opportunities by conducting a random search on your own without the capabilities offered by a real estate agent.

It is especially helpful when you enlist someone who is also knowledgeable in home valuation and factors affecting investment potential. This will assist you in making a wise financial decision when selecting your home. A real estate agent is not personally involved in the purchase. This helps you get an impartial, objective opinion about the home you are considering. It's like doing the necessary legwork in a more educated, market-wise, unbiased, efficient manner. The information and experience offered by a competent agent is a powerful tool to have on your side. Everyone should have this kind of power when searching for a home, regardless of how many homes you have purchased in the past.

The transaction portion of the purchase, that is, the financing, contracting, negotiating, closing and coordination of service individuals, is very complex. A less experienced home buyer may need more help in the transaction portion of the purchase than an experienced home buyer, but as complicated as today's real estate transactions are, a qualified real estate agent can help you in many ways. Real estate agents have been through the real estate transaction many times and are experts at dealing with the problems that can crop up at unexpected moments. A real estate agent can direct you to other qualified professionals, like home inspectors, mortgage brokers, moving companies, title companies and home insurance companies. They are experts in negotiating and in writing contracts favoring the buyer. They also know the timeline of the transaction and can guide you through each step of the purchase.

A real estate agent acting on your behalf not only will help you in the search and transaction, but also is required to help defend your best interests, including getting the lowest selling price possible. Why would an agent fight to get the lowest price, given that their commission is usually based on a percentage of the purchase price? Because most agents receive clients from their reputation and word of mouth. If your agent helped save you money and truly protected your best interests, you may refer your friends to that agent. If your agent were to save you $15,000 on the purchase price, it would mean only about $225 less in commissions for that broker, given they are paid on a 50/50 split from their real estate company. Reputation and a legal obligation to represent your best interests are worth more than that.

Things to Do

☐ Hire a competent, experienced agent who specializes in exclusive buyer representation.

☐ Be sure you are provided with all of the necessary disclosure forms and know what type of representation you are getting.

☐ Know your agent's responsibilities and discuss the ways your agent can help you find and purchase a home.

☐ Explain to your agent in detail all of your housing requirements in preparation for your search for a home.

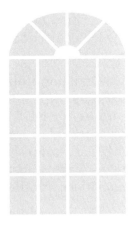

Step 4

Budgeting and the Loan Application Process

Setting a budget and applying for a loan associated with your purchase are the next important steps in buying a home. In this chapter, we'll discuss how to determine what you can afford, and illustrate both the financial requirements and the application process in securing a home mortgage. We'll also explain how to set a specific budget and jumpstart the buying process through pre-approval for a loan. First, let's discuss how you can discover what you can afford in a home and what criteria lenders specifically use in the decision to lend you money.

What Can I Afford?

Lenders use certain rules, or underwriting guidelines, to evaluate the viability of a loan. These rules may be developed in-house or stem from the Federal National Mortgage Association (FNMA) guidelines. Better known as Fannie Mae, this is the nation's largest source of mortgage funds. Created by the government in 1938, this corporation buys mortgages from lenders, re-creates them as securities and resells them to investors. This national market for mortgage debt makes it easier for buyers to borrow by the liquidity it creates.

Fannie Mae has to make the mortgage pool appealing to investors, therefore loans must conform to very specific standards. This limits the flexibility of lenders. If lenders don't write the loans as Fannie Mae specifies, they may risk being unable to resell them.

In determining how large a mortgage to grant, financial institutions will first look at the principal, interest, taxes and insurance (or P.I.T.I.) associated with the property. The principal represents the loan balance; the interest is the cost of the loan; the taxes represent the property tax figure; and insurance includes hazard insurance and possibly separate mortgage, hurricane, flood or other property damage insurance.

At this point many financial institutions will look to see how the P.I.T.I. compares to your gross income. This will establish a "debt ratio," something that lenders follow closely. The following guidelines are commonly used: The P.I.T.I. of the home should not exceed 25 to 28 percent of the applicant's gross income, and the P.I.T.I. plus other long-term debt should not exceed 33 to 36 percent of gross income.

The lender will decide to use the top or bottom of the range depending upon the size of the down payment that is made. For example, if you decide to put 10 percent down, the lender will probably use the 28 percent and 36 percent figures. If you put 5 percent down, they will use the more conservative 25 percent and 33 percent figures.

Long-term debt includes car loans, installment loans (loans that have a fixed number of payments), alimony, child support, and balances on charge cards that will take more than 10 months to pay off. Long-term debt does not include rent, utility bills, the mortgage payment on a house that is being sold to buy a new home, or payments on credit cards that are paid at the end of the month without owing interest.

In determining how much you can afford, you must calculate your monthly debt, which includes the debts listed above. Adding together all of the long-term debt will give you the monthly debt payment. To calculate the affordable house payment, take your monthly gross income, which is what you and your spouse earn in before-tax wages, and multiply this figure by .28. For example, if a couple makes $5000 monthly, they should be able to support a $1400 monthly house payment.

In determining monthly income, it is important to understand what the lenders are considering. Extra jobs are considered only if you have been working there for a year or longer. Other income, such as bonuses, commissions and overtime must be averaged over two years to be considered wages. Alimony and child-support payments are income if the payments will continue at least three years from the date of the loan application.

Now, to calculate your debt ratio, take the $1400 mortgage payment and add it to your monthly debt payment, which for the sake of this exercise, is $500. Divide this by your monthly income:

Mortgage Payment		Monthly Debt Payment		Monthly Income		Debt Ratio
$1400	+	$500	÷	$5000	=	38%

This overall debt ratio is 38 percent, exceeding normal guidelines, so some debt should be reduced before applying for a loan.

Even with debt ratios that are more conservative, there are many other reasons why a loan can be turned down. Lenders might find a poor credit history. If there is a bankruptcy or a defaulted mortgage on your record, the lender may not feel comfortable granting a new mortgage. Another reason the loan could be rejected is an unstable income source. If your income tends to fluctuate, as it would if you were paid on commission, the lender will qualify you on a conservative estimate of earnings. Lenders also will look carefully at self-employed borrowers.

Another red flag to lenders is inadequate cash reserves. If there is not enough cash in reserve to make three mortgage payments after a down payment is made, the lender may decide that you are not able to pay the debt. Cash reserves are needed in case you are laid off, become ill, or have some other rather minor financial problem that would prevent you from being able to make payments. If cash gifts are to be used as reserves, these funds need to be in your account months before applying. Lenders will verify deposits by looking at three months of your personal bank account transactions. They also will verify employment by looking at two years of W-2 statements and current paycheck stubs with year-to-date earnings. Credit also will be verified by a credit report, viewing cancelled checks and analyzing mortgage or credit card payment histories.

The better your credit is, the easier it will be for an institution to lend you money and the terms and interest rates they can offer you may be more favorable. With a better financial profile, you may also be in a position to negotiate down some of the fees that the lender may try to charge you. With this in mind, it may be a good idea to get your credit report in advance. This way you can clean up any mistakes or past debts that you may have forgotten about. Another good idea is to reduce the number of credit cards you have, even if you have no balance on them. Lenders see the credit cards as a potential risk. The way they see it, it is possible for you to go on a spending spree and be in so much debt that you can't afford the payments on your house.

Forms and More Forms:
The Application Process

Once you've decided on a lender, you will be expected to detail a great deal of personal financial information. In return, the lender is required to give you certain notices. The Real Estate Settlement and Procedures Act (RESPA) was enacted in 1974 to provide disclosure to borrowers about the costs they will incur in a real estate transaction.

RESPA requires that you receive a special information booklet from the lender no later than three days after your loan application is received. "Settlement Costs and You," by the U.S. Department of Housing and Urban Development, discusses how to negotiate a sales contract, how to work with professionals, and your rights and responsibilities as a home buyer. Lenders must also provide a Good Faith Estimate of closing costs within this time period. Included in this form will be the following information:

- Settlement charges

- Title charges

- Government recording and transfer fees

- Reserves required for deposit with the lender

- Total estimated closing costs

- Total estimated tax and insurance escrow requirements of the borrower

- Estimated loan terms

- Initial interest rate

RESPA also requires that you receive a HUD-1 settlement statement one business day prior to closing when requested. The HUD-1 is a loan settlement form that is given to the purchaser by the lender. Unlike the Good Faith Estimate, which is an estimate of *your* expenses at closing, the HUD-1 is an *exact* account of how much these items will cost and what *you and the seller* will be required to pay at closing.

Mortgage brokers are required to give you a Truth in Lending statement containing information on the annual percentage rate, the finance charge, the amount financed and the total payments required. In the case of adjustable rate loans, the total payments figure is estimated as the worst-case scenario. This statement may contain information on security interest, late charges, prepayment provisions and whether the mortgage is assumable. If you have an adjustable rate loan, it may outline the limits on the adjustments (annual and lifetime caps) and give an example of what your next year's payment might be.

The length of the loan application process varies widely, taking anywhere from seven to forty-five days to approve, depending on the complexity of the loan, the financial profile of the applicant, and the capabilities of the lender. All information regarding the loan is given to the loan processing department, where all facts connected to the buyer and the property will be investigated for accuracy.

After this, the credit report and title report are ordered. The appraisal and survey will need to be ordered later, if not already provided, to verify all the pertinent information on the property to be purchased. These reports protect the lender from the person who is a bad credit risk, or a house that is purchased for more than it is worth or that is in terrible condition, and protects the lender against any liens on the property in question.

Documents the lender may want to see include:

- Three months of your personal bank account transactions
- Two years of W-2 statements
- Current paycheck stubs with year-to-date earnings
- Credit report
- Canceled checks
- Details of mortgage or credit card payment histories
- Original purchase contract, fully executed by both buyer and seller
- Social Security card
- List of all income and assets, including detail of stocks, bonds, other securities, jewelry, boats, autos, furniture, other real estate, and life insurance policies
- List of debts and current credit card statements
- Home addresses of past two years
- Miscellaneous references
- Income tax returns, especially if self-employed
- Donor's name and address for gift letter
- Cash or check for application fee, credit report, appraisal or other expenses as necessary

A loan application form may be used similar to the one shown in the appendix. (See appendix for FNMA Uniform Residential Loan Application.)

All documents and reports are then reviewed and sent to the underwriting department, where they verify that the forms meet all of the criteria and guidelines of the investor (FHA, Fannie Mae, Freddie Mac, etc.).

You may have to decide to "float" or lock the interest rate on the loan. In floating the loan, you are deciding to wait and see if rates drop between now and a specified date. This can be a risk, because if rates rise, you may no longer qualify for the loan. By locking the loan, you are guaranteed that interest rate.

After consideration of all factors, which include the buyer's ability to pay the loan, the buyer's cash reserves, the property's value and condition, and the buyer's overall creditworthiness, the loan is approved, suspended, or denied. A suspension means an underwriter needs additional information before the loan can be approved. Once the loan is approved, the file will be transferred to the closing department where the closing date is scheduled.

Pre-Approved and Ready to Buy

As we mentioned earlier, timing is important when buying a home. Knowing when you're ready to buy has a lot to do with your present financial situation. Many first-time home buyers, regardless of how willing they are to buy, may not know whether or not they can qualify for a loan and, more importantly, what exactly they can afford. Affordability has to do with your ability to put up the initial purchase price *and* your ability to pay the ongoing expenses associated with the home.

An easy way any home buyer can find these answers is first to get pre-qualified for a loan amount, which gives you a rough estimate of how much money you can borrow. As you shop around for loan sources, any mortgage broker or lender should be able to do this for you free of charge. Then, when you choose a specific lender, you can become pre-approved for the mortgage, which involves the formal application process previously discussed.

When you are pre-approved, it means the lender has fully investigated your ability to repay a loan based on various factors, and has actually set a limit on the amount that can be spent on a home. These factors ordinarily include your income, current obligations or debt, credit history and the amount of down payment you are willing to put down for the purchase of a home. But, depending on the lender's underwriting guidelines and the type of loan being used, any number of things can affect your ability to receive approval for a loan.

Pre-approval gives you a huge advantage in the home buying game. First, you have provided the lender with up-front information about your financial situation. This eliminates any surprises about your ability to borrow and you are then able to avoid the last-minute problems that could arise.

Second, you can negotiate as though you are a cash buyer. If you find yourself in a situation where you are bidding against someone else who is not pre-approved to buy, you will have the upper hand. Your lender can supply you with a pre-qualification or pre-approval letter. One of the most common reasons real estate transactions fall through is that the buyer does not qualify for the loan to purchase the home. For this reason, sellers will be more likely to accept an offer from someone they know will not have this problem.

Third, by being pre-approved, you will be able to close sooner and move into your home more quickly. When you have completed one of the most important and time-consuming aspects of buying a home, you have also eliminated one of the primary reasons that closings are delayed.

After the loan application process is out of the way, you are ready to begin the fun stuff—working with your agent, deciding on a property type to target and hunting for your home.

Things to Do

- [ ] Select a lender and establish a specific, concrete budget to be spent on a home by becoming pre-approved for a loan.

- [ ] Start gathering all of your pertinent financial information like tax returns, W-2 statements, and bank and investment statements.

- [ ] Ask the lender or mortgage broker who pre-qualified you for a list of items they will need for final loan approval.

- [ ] If a family member is helping you with the down payment, get this money in your account at least two months prior to meeting with a lender.

- [ ] Get a credit report if there is a concern. In many instances, minor stains on your credit report can be removed easily.

- [ ] Reduce credit card and other debt as much as possible.

- [ ] Cancel a credit card or two if needed. This should also be done prior to meeting with a lender.

- [ ] Do not add to your debt with any large purchases such as a car immediately prior to this process.

- [ ] Discuss your loan status with your real estate agent. If you have a house to sell before buying, your agent should be able to help you estimate its value so that you can factor that amount into your financial picture.

Step 5

Choosing a Home That's Right for You

Now that you've selected a lender and a real estate agent, been pre-approved for a loan, and know exactly how much home you can afford, the next phase in the process of buying a home should be deciding on the type of real estate to target. This is not as easy as it sounds because there are many things to consider. Not only must you decide on design, architecture, function, construction quality and location, you must also decide how the property should be legally owned. Some of these decisions are already made for you depending on where you live and what is typical, appropriate and marketable in your area, but in most areas of the United States, there are many different property types to choose from.

In this chapter, we will help you form a picture of the type of real estate that's best for you. By understanding the options available to you when buying residential real estate, you can begin to prioritize and make a list of what matters most to you in a home. Knowing exactly what you want and need, given your personality, lifestyle, and budget, will make the eventual search for a home more efficient and effective.

Ownership Interests in Real Estate: What's Mine and What's Yours?

Real estate can be legally owned in many different ways. An individual or a group of individuals may own property. Corporations, General Partnerships, Limited Partnerships, Joint Venture Partnerships, or Real Estate Investment Trusts are examples of group ownership. Here, we will concentrate on individual ownership rights, but even these can be complicated.

The most basic and simple form of ownership is where an individual owns a property exclusively. This is commonly known as *fee simple ownership.* An individual may share fee simple ownership with others through either inheritance or survivorship rights.

Specific laws regarding the ownership of real estate vary from state to state, but basically some form of ownership exists in every state whereby these two rights, inheritance or survivorship, can be preserved. Inheritability gives an individual owner control over his or her estate. Upon an owner's death, the transfer of ownership to another is not automatic and is spelled out in the owner's will. Conversely, survivorship is an automatic right. Upon the death of an owner, the other owner automatically retains ownership of the property. Multiple owners are necessary for survivorship rights to exist.

There are many examples of inheritance or survivorship rights. *Tenancy by the Entirety* is a special form of joint tenancy for married couples where there are automatic survivorship rights. *Tenancy in Common* is where multiple owners retain undivided interest in a property and have the right to leave their share to an estate or to chosen heirs. *Joint Tenancy with Rights of Survivorship* is a type of ownership between more than one individual, where, upon the death of an owner, the surviving owner(s) automatically take over that share. *Severalty Ownership* is where a single owner has sole ownership of a piece of real estate but the estate is inheritable.

Condos, Townhouses and Co-ops

Individuals can also share ownership interests in real property with their neighbors. Common examples of real estate where ownership rights are shared are *condominiums, cooperatives* or *planned unit developments.* These phrases refer to how legal property rights are retained by the owner and have nothing to do with design, function, or architecture. A "condo" can actually refer to any type of structure.

The differences between the various categories of properties mainly have to do with the degree of shared ownership between neighboring properties and how that common ownership is divided. In general, the more exclusively the property is owned, the less restrictive the rules are on how the property can be maintained, developed and changed. The reverse is also true. The more a property is owned in common with your neighbors, the more restrictions there are.

Fee simple ownership is the most common and basic way to own real estate. Most single-family residences are owned in this way. With true fee simple ownership, the land and all permanent improvements to the land are owned outright with no common ownership being shared with neighboring properties. All care of the property is the sole responsibility of the homeowner and usually the only restrictions to the property are detailed in local building codes, zoning laws and/or deed restrictions.

Such restrictions can be extensive or limited, depending on your local government. The various restrictions may include limits on occupancy, square footage, building height, setbacks, building use, energy use, noise or behavior, and remodeling or renovation. If there is no adverse affect on neighboring properties or the well-being of the public, a homeowner can sometimes apply for a variance, or an exemption from zoning laws.

Some older fee simple properties appear to be in violation of current zoning laws, but these properties may be legally "grandfathered" in. For example, a 1920s bungalow with a garage apartment exists within an area of single family zoning. This zoning, which does not allow rental apartment structures, was established in the 1960s. Because the property was already built and the rental use was continuous, the garage apartment was automatically considered to be a "legal non-conforming use" and is approved into current zoning. Stay away from properties that are an illegal non-conforming use.

Carol and Igor, a middle-aged married couple, found that the fee simple ownership fit their life-style perfectly. They love their home and enjoy the hours spent working on the landscaping and reno-vating the kitchen and bathrooms. In the large backyard, Carol especially likes playing with her dog, and their sons like playing soccer. They had spent several years renting an apartment and the concept of not sharing a wall with someone was im-portant to them. They travel infrequently and are planning on buying more dogs, which will limit their travel plans for at least the next few years.

In a *condominium* form of ownership, an individual unit or structure is exclusively owned and undivided interest in all common areas is also retained. The area exclusively owned is usually delineated from interior wall to interior wall of the unit. An owners' association is usually set up to man-age the finances of the complex and a condominium document is used to detail the rules and regulations. Mandatory monthly or annual fees are collected to pay for the care of common components of the development. The amount of these fees will vary based on the extent of the common areas and the size of the individual unit.

Cooperative, or "co-op," ownership is similar to owning stock in a company. The share of stock you own will vary, based on the size or value of the individual unit. A proprietary lease is also executed by the owner/shareholder. The owner retains control of an individual unit, but there are usually extensive common ar-eas that are managed by an owner's association. The appeal and lifestyle of owning a property in a condominium development is similar to that of a cooperative.

Philip, a single executive, likes his new condominium. He is frequently away on business and when he is home he likes to spend his time watching sports and relaxing. The last thing he wants to do is mow a yard or landscape his property. The dues he pays monthly give him access to racquetball courts, tennis courts, a pool and fitness center. He enjoys the access to these amenities without the hassle of maintaining them. It does not bother him that he is not allowed to own a pet, put a "For Sale" sign in his own front yard or rent his condominium without approval from the condominium association. To him the convenience of condominium living is worth the few restrictions he has to endure.

A *Planned Unit Development (P.U.D.)* is sort of a cross between fee simple and condominium ownership. The phrase P.U.D. may be different throughout the United States, but basically the concept is the same. Land and improvements are owned exclusively similar to fee simple ownership. Additionally, the owner retains undivided interest in some common area. There is a homeowners' association and mandatory fees are set up to manage common areas, but care of the individual property is up to the owner. The amount and type of restrictions vary widely, based on the type of development and the degree of power given to the association.

The physical style of homes within a P.U.D. can also vary. Some are detached custom homes, but many are attached one- or two-story villas or townhouses. The term *townhouse* should be used to describe an architectural style of attached, two-story homes, not a form of ownership. It is often used incorrectly, as in a townhouse development, which is meant to describe a P.U.D.

Ace and Honey are a few years away from retirement. They still enjoy maintaining their yard and pool, and use the fitness center and clubhouse that their monthly dues help pay for. There are trees, flowers, bushes and fountains in the common areas that are maintained by the development's management, which add to the appeal of the neighborhood. They are not concerned about the restrictions, which include design approval of all houses by a board before construction can begin. They like the fact that the areas around them are well tended and that they can expect the neighborhood to continue to look as it does now.

Brownstones, as they are called in New York City, are examples of a townhouse-style residence owned in a fee simple manner without mandatory fees or common areas. As the density of units is similar to a P.U.D., the lifestyle can be much the same, but the restrictions may be fewer.

Lynda, a single professional, owns a brownstone in a busy city. She likes the convenience of being close to work so she can come home at lunch to walk her dog. She has little need of the amenities of condominium living, and would not be willing to pay the monthly dues that condominiums require. Although the yard she has is small, she enjoys tending to the areas in front and back of her brownstone. She also likes the security of having her neighbors close by in case of an emergency.

Common ownership is more prevalent in areas of higher population. This is an obvious result of land scarcity where sharing of common areas is a necessity. The low maintenance lifestyle and the ability to share in the cost, use and care of common areas are benefits many buyers enjoy. On the other hand, high monthly fees and having to answer to an owner's association may not be desirable to many individuals.

The type of ownership that's right for you depends largely on your lifestyle, your level of tolerance, and the amount of responsibility and control over the residence you would like to have. Those who are tolerant of others, have an active lifestyle, travel, and/or have little time or inclination to change, improve or care for a residence may be best suited for common ownership.

Those who want complete control over their property should aim for a fee simple type of ownership. It is difficult to generalize, however, because some condominiums have relatively few restrictions and common areas, and the owners' association may be relatively inactive and unobtrusive.

Check out the rules, regulations, deed restrictions and zoning laws associated with a residence before buying. Buyers considering purchasing property with shared ownership interests should also investigate the financial health of the development. Ask the treasurer of the homeowners' association to provide you with the development's financial statement. If there are going to be any special assessments expected in the near future, you may end up paying a large lump sum to the owners' association right after moving in. This assessment should be only a partial, prorated amount, to be split with the seller.

Investigate the tenant population in a development, especially in condos. Tenants tend to be noisier and less concerned about the condition of a unit. A higher percentage of tenants can not only make a development feel like an apartment complex, but can also drive prices down. Most condominium associations will have rules about tenants, and some may not allow tenants at all.

Form vs. Function

An obvious consideration when searching for a residence is design and architecture. In fact, what looks good is probably the first and most frequently stressed consideration when selecting a home. Buying a home that appeals to you is fine, but you shouldn't allow emotional attachment to a certain design lead you away from other considerations. The floor plan, the design and the investment potential of a home are far more important issues to bear in mind.

For example, you may have your heart set on a Mediterranean-style home. If so, make sure your search begins and ends where this style is prevalent. The design and architecture of a home should be consistent with what is within the market or target neighborhood. Also, consider whether or not the style is timeless. In other words, will the architecture of the home still be popular and marketable in the future? Always think about the resale potential of a home. Everyone knows of a home in his or her area that looks like a "Brady Bunch home" or something right out of the late 1960s. Ideally, you should not be able to tell when a home was built unless, of course, you are buying a home with historical significance.

You should not let your personal taste in design get in the way of a smart investment choice. Try to choose a style that you will like and one that the general population will like as well. You have to be unselfish and sensitive to the desires of the market. For example, avoid selecting a geodesic dome house in a traditional neighborhood.

The functional utility of the home, or the usefulness of the floor plan, is an important item to consider and is closely related to the design of a home. Understanding what's best for you is more complex than just choosing a bedroom/bath count. An easy way to understand functional utility is to look at a floor plan drawing of a home. Are the rooms positioned in a logical way? Is there a good flow from room to room? Is there a smart ratio of bedrooms to baths to living areas? As a rule, there should never be more bathrooms or living areas than bedrooms. It should never be necessary to go through one bedroom to get to another. Ceiling heights, sizes of rooms and positions of interior walls should also be considered.

Appraisers refer to *incurable functional obsolescence*, which simply refers to a situation where the money necessary to fix a property's problem exceeds the value that investment adds to a home. Curable problems are those that can be easily fixed, with the money invested being less than the value it adds to the property. Look for incurable problems in a home when shopping. For example, homes with serious floor plan problems, such as having only one bathroom in a five-bedroom house, should be avoided. Other homes may have serious foundation problems that negatively impact the entire structure. Obviously, the cost to cure this problem would exceed the value it would add.

On the other hand, if removal of an interior wall could greatly increase the utility and appeal of a home, you may still consider buying the property because the cost of removing the wall may be relatively small. Smart investors actually look for minor, curable problems when shopping for bargains in real estate. The theory is that these curable problems are mainly cosmetic or easily fixed with relatively little investment and these defects actually keep other potential buyers away from making a competitive offer on the home.

There will never be a home with perfect form or function. Every home has at least one problem or defect, so understanding which problems are curable and which problems will cause a real financial setback is vital to your investment strategy. Your appraiser or your real estate agent should be able to help you identify which is a curable or incurable defect, and, for that matter, which home improvements will actually add to the value of the home.

Location, Location, Location

You have probably heard the phrase, "location, location, location," so you may be tempted to go to the best neighborhood possible and see what you can afford. Many buyers soon come to the realization that the only affordable properties in the better neighborhoods are the type that you wouldn't be happy living in. While it is true that location is more important than the home itself, at some point you have to decide whether the home is at least minimally livable and comfortable. You can fix a home, but you can't fix a neighborhood. However, there's still that minor detail called a budget that you have to consider.

For those searching for a single-family home, the debate becomes: "How much emphasis should I give to location vs. the quality of the home?" In other words, how much of your budget should go towards land value (or location) and how much should go towards the improvement value (or home)? Many banks have strict guidelines regarding the percentage of value in land vs. improvements when lending money. Their underwriters don't like the land value to exceed 30 percent of the property's total value. In reality, properties in better, more established neighborhoods, or those with water or golf course frontage, have a land value of more than 50 percent of their total value.

Regardless of the property type, you will need to pay for a good location. Investing in a good location will offer the best return on your investment. The best way to approach this issue is to decide what property type, design and floor plan will offer the bare minimum in functional utility and comfort. This will offer some guidelines for evaluating the cost of the home alone. Then you can decide how much of your budget you can allocate to land or location. Estimating average land values in a specific area can help you select a neighborhood that's right for you. Shoot for the best neighborhood possible, given the remainder of the budget.

Separating the structure's value from the land value is a good way to understand affordability when choosing a location. A *cost approach* to value can help you do this. (See Step 7). By multiplying the square footage of the heated living area by a dollar figure representing the cost to build new, a value of the structure can be calculated. An allowance should be given for the depreciation or effective age of the structure, and an amount needs to be added for land value or any non-living area improvements like garages or pools. This may be difficult to do if these structures are owned in common with other owners. Your agent or real estate appraiser should be able to help with this approach.

When a search for a home begins, the goal should be to find the best neighborhood you can afford with the type of residence that has the minimum utility and construction quality you want. You must also look for homes that have the design and architectural style that is consistent with other homes in the area. That way, even if the property is purchased at market value, chances are the property will appreciate.

Another option is to build a new home based on your exact needs. Buying vacant land or tearing down highly depreciated homes for the land value will give you a more exact idea of what you can spend on the construction of a home and improvements. More will be discussed about new construction later.

Things to Do

☐ Investigate ownership interests in real estate and consider which one best suits you.

☐ Consider the idea of common ownership and how that will fit into your lifestyle and personality.

☐ Consider your needs with respect to both form and function. Go to the bookstore or library to pick up magazines or books that offer floor plans and architectural options. Visit as many residences as possible. Both older homes and new model residences can give you ideas. Watch television programs that deal with design and architecture.

☐ Begin to formulate an idea of your perfect home and your perfect neighborhood. Drive through neighborhoods and begin to specify where you may want to live. Look at residential styles within those neighborhoods. Soon you will need to explain these housing requirements in detail to your real estate agent.

Step 6

House Hunting and Your Home's Investment Potential

Now that you have a very specific idea of what you want in a home, you can start searching. For most people, the purchase of a home is the single largest investment of their life. You should view it as an investment, first and foremost. Unfortunately many buyers do not do this, mostly because they don't understand the factors affecting real estate value. It's everyone's goal to get a great buy on their home. However, future value potential or *the appreciation of the property over time* is what buyers really need to be concerned with.

As the old saying goes, it is just as easy to fall in love with a rich person as it is to fall in love with a poor person. Well, this is actually the way you should approach buying a home. You can fall in love with a home that is a good investment just as easily as you can fall in love with a home that is a bad investment. You should love your home, but you should also think of the long-term financial implications of the choices you make when purchasing the home. Again, remember to think of the home as an investment first. Let's consider some tips that can help.

Hunting Efficiently: Locating the Best Home in the Least Amount of Time

According to the National Association of Realtors survey, "The Home Buying and Selling Process 1997," the typical home buyer searched a median of eight weeks to find the home ultimately purchased, and examined a median number of 10 homes. The time it takes to find a home can take days or many months, depending on your housing needs, the availability of residences, and how efficiently you conduct your search.

Finding a home has a lot to do with being aware of opportunities, acting fast when that opportunity arises, and beating competitive buyers to the punch. With today's Multiple Listing Service and the advanced computer systems used to search listings, your agent has the capability of making you aware of every home actively listed for sale that suits your needs.

Having specified certain search parameters, current on-line systems can even show digital pictures of your potential home from a computer screen. Many times a home listed for sale can be eliminated from your search without even visiting the property. These systems can even offer photos of neighboring homes and street scenes. Public records can also be accessed, offering other pertinent information, like previous purchase prices and property taxes.

Explain in detail to your agent your housing requirements and request that you be provided with all applicable new listings on a frequent basis. View these homes routinely. Use your real estate agent as your only information source on new listings. Internet sites that detail only a certain company's listings do not cover all of the available housing possibilities. Your agent will have access to those same listings and will specify only those homes that are right for you. Do not look in the newspaper or drive the streets randomly looking for homes. Driving around to get a feel for a neighborhood in general is fine, as long as you do not concern yourself with specific "for sale" signs. This is a waste of time. If you find a house on your own and the house is not on the list provided by your agent, chances are some aspect of the home does not suit your needs. For example, the home may be out of your price range or may not have enough bathrooms. The goal is to find a home that suits all of your needs, not just a few.

Only about 10 percent of all sales are For Sale by Owner or "F.S.B.O." As a general rule, beware of these homes. Sellers not represented by an agent tend to overprice their homes, lack objectivity, may not be serious about selling and generally may not know what they are doing. Purchasing a F.S.B.O. *is not a way to save money.* By selling on their own and saving commissions, sellers do not pass the savings on to you as the buyer. Why should they? It is a common misconception that you get a better deal by targeting a F.S.B.O. In fact, you most likely will spend too much money because the seller's asking price is usually inflated.

Without the knowledge of comparable market data, many people think their home is worth more than it is. This is a case of perception vs. reality. It's like going to a factory outlet mall, hoping for a bargain because you think you are cutting out the middleman. In reality, the prices may be the same or higher. The transaction may also take longer and be more costly because you're dealing with a seller less experienced in selling a home. Legal issues, title and repair problems may also arise and, unlike a real estate professional, the owners don't have the expertise to handle these issues.

Once in a great while you can find a good deal with a F.S.B.O. mainly because sellers don't know what their home is worth. They do under price their homes on occasion, so being aware of what is a good value in a certain area is important. Your agent or real estate appraiser can be an enormous benefit in this area. Real estate agents can still represent you in a F.S.B.O. transaction, but may be paid out of the proceeds of closing or on an hourly basis. Most sellers are still willing to pay a 2- to 3-percent commission to the buyer's agent. This should be discussed during your initial conversations with the agent.

Many buyers also believe foreclosures are another way of finding a bargain. Because of this misconception, there are actually more competitive buyers drawn to bidding on foreclosures. The truth is that most foreclosures are actually purchased at or above market value! This bargain hunting frenzy actually drives the price up, and foreclosures usually are the properties that need the most work. Not only are buyers paying top dollar, but extensive renovations are often required.

Buying at auction is also a risk. Depending on how the auction is conducted, the property may have problems that can't be detected prior to purchase. As properties are purchased "as is," clear title or structural soundness can't be guaranteed. Bargain hunting competitive buyers also may drive the price up over market value.

As you visit homes for sale, ask questions but say nothing positive out loud to the seller or the seller's agent. Keep a real poker face. Acting desperate to buy can be used against you in the negotiation process. Your agent will have paperwork on each home you visit. This may include pictures, public records, Multiple Listing Service fact sheets, floor plans or surveys of the homes. Make notes on the positive and negative aspects of each home. Picture yourself living in the home.

Most homes can be ruled out before even going inside. Look at neighboring houses. Remember that these next-door neighbors' homes can affect the value of the home you are considering. If possible, interview the neighbors. This will give you more information about the community, the seller's situation and the neighbor's personality. This could be your neighbor someday, so it's important.

Consider the general location of the home and its proximity to schools, shopping and other important support facilities. Don't be afraid to re-visit a home that shows potential. Try to view the home during the day and at night. You will get a different perspective, since properties can look different at various times and you may have missed something the first time around.

As you search, keep in mind you will likely give up something you now consider important. You might decide that a gourmet kitchen is not as crucial as you thought it was. Keep in mind the things you *must* have, such as a garage, a second bathroom or a third bedroom. Prioritize by making a list of desirable items in order of importance. Don't get bogged down in details. Don't consider whether your furniture will fit in a certain room. Throw out your tape measure. Don't rule out a good deal because your $150 couch won't fit in a room.

If you have searched for a while but can't find your dream home, your agent can also help you locate building lots and builders. You can build a new home to the exact specifications you would like. Many new developments feature packages where the builder acts as a developer as well. You can buy the land and building in one package and use a construction loan to finance the deal.

Dealing with a builder is similar to dealing with another seller, except price is not as negotiable. Especially with larger builders, prices are normally pre-set and are based on standard model designs. Most builders will cooperate with real estate agents and will pay their commission, which is usually 2 to 4 percent of the cost to build. If you show up at a builder's office without an agent, you will not receive a discount for the commission. So it can be helpful to you as a buyer to have your agent helping you through this process as well.

Another option is to find a highly depreciated home in a good location and tear it down. Tear-downs are becoming more and more popular as desirable neighborhoods are becoming more and more built-up. Vacant parcels in those neighborhoods can be hard to find and properties with older, poorly kept homes can sell for the same price as vacant parcels. Sometimes these homes rest on two or more buildable lots. If the zoning permits, tearing down one home can offer the ability to build two or more homes. Some smart buyers do this and completely fund their land purchase by selling off the extra parcel. Ask your agent to look for homes like this if vacant parcels are not available.

Whatever route you choose, be patient. The process of actually finding a home that is a good investment takes time.

20 Ways to Maximize Investment Potential When Choosing Your Home

The following tips will help you choose and purchase a home that can be sold someday for a big profit. Remember, if you're buying a home with resale value in mind, there are some rules to follow. Obviously, you may not meet all of these guidelines, but if you want to own a great investment, try for as many as possible. We suggest that you:

(1) *Buy the least valuable home on the block.* The Economic Theory of Conformity states that values tend to conform to the median or average sales price within the market. When most of the homes in your neighborhood are of a higher value than your own, your home's value will tend to rise at a greater rate than if it was located in a neighborhood of lesser-valued homes. If you buy the most valuable home in the neighborhood, the home may still go up in value, but at a much lesser rate. This rule tends to hold true for any property type. We're not saying you should buy a poor quality home or a home so small that it is not marketable. Just be concerned with the size, condition and construction quality of the homes immediately surrounding the home under consideration and never buy a home that is over-improved for the neighborhood.

(2) *Hire a real estate agent.* Buying a home is becoming more and more complex. Think of the paperwork, inspections, negotiations and financing. Without an agent, how will you access the up-to-date information of *all* actively listed properties for sale? How will you efficiently conduct a search for a home? Do you have the time necessary to find the right property at the right price? A real estate agent can effectively help you find a home and help you through each step of the process. And, the seller is the one traditionally responsible for paying the fee for this service! You have nothing to lose.

(3) *Hire a real estate agent who is competent and specializes in buyer representation.* This is crucial. Inexperienced and incompetent real estate salespersons are out there, so be careful to choose an agent who is college educated, experienced and spe-

cializes in buyer representation. A buyer's agent is the one that is expert in the needs of the buyer and is required to fight for the buyer's best interests, including negotiating the lowest possible sales price. Never buy from a seller's agent or a dual agent, as there might be a conflict of interest.

(4) *Buy residences with minor cosmetic defects*. Homes that have minor defects can be cleaned up with minimal expense. These defects will keep other, less knowledgeable buyers from making competitive offers and can drive the price down to bargain levels. Bidding wars tend to occur on homes that are in perfect shape. Consider the cost to cure the problems of a home and don't pass up a good deal because of a minor defect. Focus on the potential of a home. The small money and effort you put into the cosmetics of the home could pay large dividends when reselling.

(5) *Avoid homes with major structural damage or adverse conditions*. A home inspection will identify if the home has major structural damage. Major repairs can translate into major money out the window. Foundation, roof or other structural problems are the most common reasons people lose money when repairs are necessary. Also watch out for "toxic homes," where lead paint, radon gas or asbestos causes a health hazard. Avoid homes where street noise or outdoor foul odors are prevalent. Make sure your contract lets you walk away if the home is unsound in any way. Know the cost of repairs and have these estimates included in the inspection report. Also know the "Remaining Economic Life" of the property component, or the amount of time remaining before the item needs replacing. If something big needs replacing during your ownership period, it still translates into big expense for you. (See Step 8 for further details.)

(6) *Look for motivated sellers*. A motivated seller will be ready to bargain with you. When an owner relocates or lives out of town, dies, becomes ill, has already bought another home, gets a divorce, has family members leaving or entering the home, has financial difficulties, or has had his home on the market for a long time, there may be a motivation to sell. Try to find out why

the seller is selling. Simply ask the seller or ask a neighbor. Refuse to make an offer until you know the reason the property is for sale. Claim you are fearful of buying someone else's problems. A less urgent selling situation can mean less room for negotiation and a higher sales price.

(7) *Buy a home located in a neighborhood with a history of strong appreciation in value.* Your real estate agent will probably know the areas that appreciate the most and can find recent sales in any area you choose. County property tax records are available to anyone and will show you what an owner originally paid for his or her home. This is a good way to measure how much, if at all, a home has appreciated in value. If an individual home has no history of previous sales, as with newer construction, its general neighborhood sales history can be a reliable indicator of price appreciation. Past trends of appreciation don't always guarantee that a certain rate will continue in the future. Yet, most of the time the recent rate of neighborhood appreciation continues into a buyer's ownership period. On average, expect anywhere from 3- to 10-percent rates. Anything above 5 percent is terrific.

(8) *Be less concerned with getting a bargain and be more concerned with a property's potential for future appreciation.* The resale value, or the future sales price of your home, may be more important than the original purchase price of the property when considering your total return on investment. Chances are you will not find a quality home for too much under market value, anyway, even if the seller is motivated. If a property goes up in value, it means the property is marketable and will be sold at market value.

However, most people want a bargain. Consider Stephanie, who buys a home at market value. The home then appreciates $20,000 in value in three years. Now consider Bill, who buys a property for $5,000 under market value, yet that home appreciates only $5,000 in three years. Stephanie has netted $20,000, while Bill is up only $10,000. And this rate of appreciation is likely to continue for both as long as they own their properties!

(9) *Buy a home in the heart of the action.* Scarcity is another major concept of value. When there's a limited supply relative to the demand for a type of product, like waterfront or certain downtown properties, the product will be marketable and its value will rise. Consider what makes a home marketable: location, location, location. For example, the most central, exclusive areas of New York City, San Francisco, Los Angeles, Boston, Philadelphia, and the waterfront areas of, well, just about any place, are greatly appreciating in value. Future buyers of your home want to be in the center of a great location.

(10) *Buy a home with a timeless, popular design or architecture.* Avoid stressing your own personal preferences if they are different from the norm. The funky home you want now could look dated when you try to resell it. You could lose thousands of dollars on a design that only you could love. Again, think marketability. You want to appeal to the masses, and the majority of people are drawn to popular, timeless designs and architecture. If you dare to be different, don't do it with the biggest investment of your life.

(11) *Buy a home with a logical, functional floor plan.* The utility of a home, or its ability to satisfy a person's housing needs, is important. Look out for low ceilings, choppy, small rooms, having to go through one bedroom to get to another, and disproportionate numbers of bedrooms to bathrooms to living areas. Think of what is functional, logical and appealing. Open, bright areas and spacious vaulted ceilings should be popular for years to come. You'll be happier in the long run with a home that has a sensible floor plan, and you'll satisfy the needs of future buyers of your home.

(12) *Appraise the home before you make an offer.* Why not? You will have to get an appraisal of the property before the lender will approve your application for a loan. Why not know in advance what to offer? An offer should never be based on the seller's list price, but on *your* estimate of market value. Although you should be less concerned with getting a bargain if a property has great investment potential, you don't want to pay too much for a property.

Having the information that an appraisal gives you is priceless during the negotiation process. If getting an appraisal is not possible, at least have your real estate agent do a Comparative Market Analysis or pull some comparable sales for you.

(13) *Buy a home that will be suitable for you and your family in the future.* Plan on future needs. This prevents major expense in renovations and upgrades over time. Buy a home you can grow into. Even though two bedrooms may be suitable now, a four-bedroom home may be needed before you know it. The cost of adding a wing to a home may prevent future resale profit. Once you've made your purchase, upgrade or change the residence only with improvements that will boost value. This will be discussed further in the last chapter.

(14) *Be in a position to act fast, because smart money deals go quickly.* Before you start your search for a home, make sure you are in a position to make an offer immediately if necessary. Your dream home could be the first one you see, and if it's a good deal, other buyers will know it. Remember that you are in competition with other buyers who are ready to snatch a good deal away from you. Be ready financially, know what you want, and be able to respond to your agent when a new home listing comes on the market. Remember to be pre-approved for a loan amount. Be decisive and either go for it or forget about the home and move on to the next one. New listings and good deals appear every day, so be ready.

(15) *Prioritize and concentrate on the major aspects of a home.* Don't get caught up in all the little details of a home and let its most important aspects be a lesser priority. Realize that no home will have everything you want. Location, square footage, year built, construction quality and architectural design are more important than the color of the walls or whether your furniture will fit in the home. Don't pass up a good deal because of a couch or minor imperfections in a home that can be easily changed at little expense. Get the big picture.

(16) *Avoid homes involved in a bidding war.* You may always be in competition with other buyers, but if more than one

party is bidding on a home at the same time, the price can be driven up above market value. Know the maximum amount to spend, and avoid homes, no matter how attractive, that are involved in a bidding war. Buy with your head, not your heart. Buying frenzies tend to happen when people fall in love with a particular home, forgetting that there are many other homes out there to buy.

(17) *Select a home with good access or proximity to quality support facilities, like good schools, shopping and recreation.* Sending the kids to a good school and easy access to shopping or recreation is obviously important. This may mean the home is located either in close proximity to these support facilities, or easy access is possible by way of car, train or other form of transportation. Therefore, a more rural home can still be marketable if a major highway is nearby or the home is within a good school district. Make sure the roads leading to the home are in good shape and paved. Test the roads by driving from the home to downtown, schools and shopping. In real estate, a property's accessibility is sometimes referred to as a "linkage" and is a major factor in strong resale potential.

(18) *Be aware of future growth plans for the neighborhood.* We've mentioned the importance of analyzing past trends of appreciation within a neighborhood as a way of possibly predicting future investment potential, but you should also be aware of an area's plans for the future. Know if a neighborhood will soon undergo rezoning, if new residential construction is about to begin nearby, or if a new highway, shopping mall or school is being planned. These events can have a positive or negative affect on the value of your home.

Know your neighborhood's current phase of development. The transitional phases of a neighborhood are the *development phase* (new construction, occurs during the first year to ten years), the *stability phase* (occurs during the next ten to fifty years), the *digression phase* (lasts ten to twenty years), and the *restoration phase* (lasts five to twenty years or more). The only phase to avoid when buying is the *digression phase,* as it is characterized by a decline in the condition and values of properties. Tear-downs or extensive renovation projects occur within a neighborhood during the restoration phase, and are good signs that the area's land value is rising. If you buy in the direction of positive growth, even a more rural property that presently breaks all the rules mentioned can be a great area for investment. John Jacob Astor was one of the first people in America to strike it rich in real estate by buying land in the direction of growth. He bought mostly unwanted farmland in Manhattan in the early 1800s, just outside of the already developed areas. As development and demand grew into the areas owned by Astor, so did his wealth.

(19) *Know present market conditions and interest rates.* Is this a buyer's market or a seller's market? This shouldn't affect whether or not you buy or the timing of your purchase, because it is impossible to predict what the real estate market will do in the future. Yet, it should affect how much you offer. Know present market conditions. If you're in a buyer's market, your offer can be lower than normal because there is a surplus of homes from which to choose. If it takes less than an average of 45 days to sell a home in a given neighborhood or the gap between the average list price and selling price is less than five percent, you are probably in a seller's market. Be aware of interest rates as well. If rates are low, then even in a seller's market a buyer may be able to afford the higher price of homes.

(20) *Look for homes with a great view.* A beautiful view sells. No matter what location, if the view is terrific, the home will be more marketable. And the better the view, the higher the price. Consider two highrise condo units with the same floor plan—the one on a higher floor facing the ocean will sell for more than the one on a lower floor facing the parking lot every time. A townhome high on a hill in San Francisco, a ski mountain retreat in Colorado, a beach house in Malibu, or a Fifth Avenue co-op overlooking Central Park in New York City all have hefty price tags that will be even heftier tomorrow.

Case Studies:
How to and How Not to Buy a Home

The following are real life examples of two couples' experience in purchasing their homes and the long-term investment implications of their purchases. This is based on two actual deals. Both couples had similar budgets, were successful, professional newlyweds, around 30 years old, and were about to begin their lives together. One couple did not follow most of the tips listed previously, the other couple did. Here are their stories.

The Smiths

Newly married, successful and ready to buy, the Smiths hire a friend of the family to act as their agent. This agent works part-time and has little experience in buyer representation, real estate finance or valuation, but does manage to establish a good rapport. There was never a discussion about the couple's future housing needs or the factors that affect the investment potential of real estate.

With a budget of $300,000, the agent shows them a few homes, but really begins to push one in particular. It's a home she has listed where she is also acting as the agent for the seller. It's a home she's familiar with, and she'll have the opportunity to receive both ends of the commission. Her sales pitch finally works, and the couple eventually agrees to pay the full $300,000 asking price for the home.

The home, a large, 3,900-square-foot frame residence, was built in the 1940s and rests on three buildable lots. It is by far the largest house on the block, but their agent kept insisting it was a bargain, based on a dollar-per-square-foot calculation. The homes immediately adjacent are about half the size of the couple's home in living area and land. The home consists of a huge living room, a family room, a den, a small kitchen, two bedrooms and two baths. Nearby is a busy street, and traffic noise is clearly heard. No property inspection was performed before closing, since the property was in good shape cosmetically.

Soon after purchase, the Smiths welcome their first baby. Not long after, a large portion of the roof falls in, termite damage is found and the foundation shifts. Repairs are made. Soon, baby number two is born. With two children, the need for more bedrooms becomes evident, and the couple decides to build a new wing with two new bedrooms. They then decide that the facade surrounding the entry should be enhanced. Tinting for the windows and a pool with a spa is added. The busy street nearby was also widened by the city, making traffic noise even louder.

The home ends up to be 4,500 square feet of living area with a pool. The cost of repairs and renovations to the home has totaled $150,000. The day-to-day maintenance of the property is expensive and calls for many miscellaneous contractors over the years.

Seven years after the original purchase, they sell the home for $395,000. Without even factoring in financing, maintenance and closing costs, they lose $55,000. Here's the math:

Sales Price	$395,000
Original Purchase Price	$300,000
Repairs and Renovations	$150,000
Return	($ 55,000)—Loss

The Joneses

Also newly married and successful, Mr. & Mrs. Jones have a similar budget of $300,000. They hire an experienced, college-educated agent who specializes in exclusive buyer representation. After understanding the couple's present and future needs and discussing real estate as an investment, the agent takes them to several properties recently put on the market. None of the listings are their agent's listings, as she never represents sellers.

After an extensive search, the couple decides to make an offer on a four-bedroom, two-and-one-half-bath home. Built in 1960, the 2,400-square-foot home is on a deep-water canal with a beautiful view and is surrounded by larger homes. The seller, an architect who lives out of state, recently completed construction on a new wing and a screen-enclosed pool and spa for the home. Tenants who occupied the home moved out due to divorce. The brick home needs general clean-up and cosmetic renovation, but is solid and passed all structural tests in the inspection. The landscaping needs work and the kitchen and bathrooms need updating.

The seller is desperate to sell, as his monthly payment on the home is no longer covered by rent. The Joneses' agent negotiates a deal that would call for the seller to make all functional repairs. The agent also urges the couple to have the home appraised, which they do. The agent pulls a sales history on the home. Their initial offer is below the asking price, matching what the seller originally paid for the home before renovations. The final sales price is between the appraised value and the seller's original purchase price of four years earlier — $225,000. A combination of the seller's motivation, a good agent fighting for a low sales price, and knowledge of market value helped secure a below-market price.

After closing, Mr. & Mrs. Jones began renovating the kitchen, baths and landscaping. No major structural repairs or room additions were ever necessary, even after they used a bedroom as a home-office. The total cost of renovation was $30,000. The homes in the popular area began growing even bigger, due to neighbors renovating or tearing down old homes and building new.

Six years after their original purchase, the couple sells their home for $670,000. Without factoring in financing, maintenance and closing costs, they gained $415,000. Here's the math:

Sales Price	$670,000
Original Purchase Price	$225,000
Repairs and Renovations	$ 30,000
Return	$415,000—Gain

With similar budgets and at a similar time in their lives, Mr. & Mrs. Smith lost $55,000 after seven years and Mr. & Mrs. Jones gained $415,000 after six years. The financial ramifications of their home purchases are enormous. The real estate agents are as responsible as the buyers for these results. Stories like these continue to happen to buyers every day.

Things to Do

☐ Conduct efficient home searches frequently and routinely.

☐ Make notes and re-visit homes that show potential. Try to specify the one home that is best for you, and be prepared to act fast with an offer if necessary.

☐ Talk to your agent about real estate as an investment. Discuss the tips mentioned in this chapter. Make sure that you are willing to consider only those homes for sale that are a good investment.

Step 7

Real Estate Valuation

By now you've found a home that you like and believe will be a good investment. It's time to consider its market value in preparation for making an offer. Have you chosen a home that is priced right and is a good value? Is the asking price reasonable and based on comparable market data? As your offer should be based on *your* conclusion of market value, not the seller's, an understanding of real estate appraisal is vital.

Real estate sales agents who also have some experience in real estate valuation can help you enormously. Also, consult a state-certified residential real estate appraiser for advice. They are the best people to tell you about the real estate valuation process and a home's investment potential.

What's This Home Really Worth?

Understanding the true market value of a product is important no matter what you're buying, since this should be the basis of your offer. When you initially present a contract to the seller, the suggested sales price should never be based on the seller's list price. A seller or a seller's agent probably established this price, and they might not have any idea how to conclude market value. Their price may be wildly inflated or under market value. Either way, your estimate is what's important — not theirs.

Real estate appraisers estimate market value, which is defined as the most likely sales price of real estate as of a specified date, given a typically motivated and educated seller and buyer. In this definition, it is also implied that the seller should be able to transfer the title to you free and clear, the property has been on the market for a reasonable time and the terms of the sale are all cash in U.S. dollars or the equivalent.

For most people outside of the real estate business, the value of a residence is difficult to estimate, mostly due to a lack of local market information and knowledge regarding the real estate valuation process. Homebuyers who are new to an area may still be thinking of the home prices of their old neighborhood. For example, if a New Yorker relocates to Florida and believes all the real estate prices in the Sunshine State are a bargain, then he or she may pay too much for a home.

To avoid paying more than local market value, you can ask your real estate agent to do a *comparative market analysis* (CMA) or simply ask him to pull some comparable sales for you. This is a less accurate way to find your home's value because real estate agents are not always experts in home appraisal, but you will have a better idea of what the market will bear, based on real comparable sales data.

Never rely on a "dollar per square foot" number to estimate value. Some real estate agents love this method, probably because it's so easy to do and it's the only way they know how to appraise a home. But simply dividing a sales price by the heated square footage of a home is far too simple — and inaccurate — and does not account for other important components of a property, like lot size, depreciation, location, view, construction quality, design, car storage, sheds, pools or any other non-living area improvement.

A more accurate option is to hire a state-certified residential real estate appraiser to estimate a property's value before making an offer to purchase. This can help give some peace of mind to a buyer who is uncertain what to offer for a particular piece of property. A buyer is normally required to pay for a real estate appraisal during the loan process anyway. A lender will need a state-certified residential real estate appraisal to approve your loan, so getting an appraisal done before the offer can kill two birds with one stone. Paying the typical appraisal fee prior to an offer is better than overpaying thousands of dollars in purchase price.

Please note that a state-certified appraisal cannot be performed by your real estate agent, even if that agent holds a state-certified residential appraisal license. An appraisal is supposed to be written by an independent, unbiased third party with no present or future interest in the property being appraised. It could be construed that your agent has an interest in the property, as a commission may result from the transaction.

Also note that an appraiser acts as a market researcher, not a building inspector. Many assumptions are made when writing an appraisal, and these are spelled out in the Limiting Conditions pages of the report. (See appendix for Statement of Limiting Conditions and Appraiser's Certification.) An appraiser usually does not test all of the various systems of the house like a building inspector does, and may assume that the home is functional if no damage is visible during the inspection. Make sure the building inspection is consistent with the descriptions within the appraisal report.

Sometimes buyers and sellers decide to base the contract price on the appraised value of the residence. In other words, the sales price is decided only after the appraisal is performed. This may mean buying a property for retail value, but it avoids a lot of the negotiation process. Remember that paying retail or market value for a property is not a bad thing if the property goes way up in value over time.

It's important for the buyer to choose the appraiser and then have the seller approve that choice. You do not want a friend of the seller deciding what you should pay for a home. Some choose to have two appraisals performed and then average the two estimates of value. Relocation companies often require three appraisals to be performed when selling a transferred employee's home.

The sales price of the home is based on the middle appraised value. In other words, the high and low appraised values are not used. After all, an appraisal is a subjective opinion of value.

With this in mind, let's talk about the three approaches state-certified real estate appraisers use to estimate a property's value.

Income, Cost and Market: The Three Certified Approaches to Value

In a state-certified residential real estate appraisal, there are three ways, or approaches, to estimate the market value of a home. They are known as the *Income Approach*, the *Cost Approach* and the *Market Approach* (a.k.a. the *Sales Comparison Approach*).

The Income Approach

The *Income Approach* is used for income-producing or rental properties. Here, rent or income of a property is used to conclude value. There are two methods of using an Income Approach to value.

The first method, sometimes called a *Rental Index*, is where estimated annual or monthly rent of a property is multiplied by a GIM (Gross Income Multiplier, typically used with yearly rent), or a GRM (Gross Rent Multiplier, typically used with monthly rent) to estimate market value. For example, on a monthly basis, properties with a gross monthly rent of $800 and a GRM of 100 would be valuated at $80,000 ($800 x 100). A multiplier is established by averaging the multipliers of at least three comparable rental properties.

This is the least reliable of the approaches to value for most residential properties, as rent multipliers are sometimes questionable and vary widely, as they are derived from local market conditions. Rent numbers may also be inaccurate and may not allow for vacancy and other expenses. Understanding market rent is useful, however, as owners may have to rent their residence to cover their mortgage payments or may want to use the residence as a source of positive cash flow.

The second method is more involved but more accurate and utilizes a capitalization method. Called the *Income Capitalization Approach*, market value is estimated based on the present worth of future income from the property.

In this approach, net income is divided by a capitalization rate to conclude present market value. Net income must first be estimated. Expenses such as vacancy and collection losses, taxes, insurance, management fees, insurance, repairs and replacements are subtracted from annual gross income. Let's say an annual net income of $15,000 is concluded and a capitalization rate acceptable to investors of 13 percent is used. The present market value would be $115,385. ($15,000 divided by .13). (See appendix for a sample of a Small Residential Income Property Appraisal Report.)

The Cost Approach

The *Cost Approach* to value estimates the reproduction cost of a property by placing a dollar figure on its individual components. This approach is sometimes called the *Comparative Square Foot Method* or *Cost-Depreciation Method.*

A dollar-per-square-foot amount, or cost to build new, is multiplied by the heated square footage of the structure. Depreciation, which is the loss of value for any reason such as physical deterioration, is subtracted after adding other items that are individually valued like pools and site improvements. Land is then added onto the depreciated value of the improvements. The following is a simple example:

2,100 sq. ft. living area X	$55 per square foot =	$115,500
483 sq. ft. garage X	$25 per square foot =	$ 12,075
Extras (pool, shed, site improvements)		$ 20,000
Cost new of improvements		$147,575
Depreciation allowance		$ 14,758
Subtotal (depreciated value of improvements)		$132,817
Land value		$ 40,000
Total value		**$172,817**

The Cost Approach to value is somewhat unreliable for older residences, as depreciation and cost to build numbers become more difficult to estimate. However, this is a good way to separate land value from improvement value.

The *Quantity Survey Method* is another form of the Cost Approach to value and involves a more detailed inventory of all costs, including labor, materials, builder's profit and other indirect costs. This method is great for new construction and really shows a breakdown of all individual expenses related to the cost to build a property.

The *Unit-In-Place Method* is a less detailed and simpler way of estimating the cost to build a structure. Also good for new construction, this technique estimates the cost of each component part of a structure. For example, a contractor will quote the cost per square foot of hardwood floors with labor, materials and polyurethane finish included. The square feet of flooring multiplied by this estimate would be the cost of the job.

The Market Approach

The *Market Approach*, also known as the *Sales Comparison Approach*, is the most commonly used and most reliable approach to value for residential properties. Three or more recent sales of homes similar to the subject property are analyzed. The sales prices of the comparable sales are adjusted to allow for property differences in comparison to the subject property being appraised.

There are many forms used in real estate appraisal, but the one you probably need to order is a Fannie Mae Form 1004, or a Uniform Residential Appraisal Report. This is the form most often used for single family residences, but you should verify which form would be used in association with your home loan before ordering an appraisal. In the Market Approach section of this form, adjustments are made to allow for differences in financing, sale date, location, site size, view, design, construction quality, age, condition, room count, living area, unfinished rooms, functional utility, heating and cooling, energy efficient items, car storage, porches, pools or other extras.

The prices of the comparable sales are adjusted to reflect these differences. These adjusted prices are then averaged or an individual adjusted value is stressed and an appraised value is concluded. The more adjustments that are made, the less comparable the sale is to the subject property. The more valid and comparable the sales are, the more reliable the estimate of value is. Finding truly comparable sales is the best way to understand the value of a residence.

Within the report is a section for each of the three approaches to value. Appraisers usually stress the one approach judged to be the most reliable. With single family home appraisals, the Market Approach is usually given the most consideration. (See appendix for a sample of a Uniform Residential Appraisal Report and an Individual Condominium Unit Appraisal Report.)

Choosing the Right Real Estate Appraiser

Ask for an appraiser's company brochure, resume or web site address. Be sure the appraiser is State-Certified Residential. In most states, those appraisers who hold a state-certified residential license have at least two calendar years of experience, have completed a minimum number of reports and hours of appraisal coursework, are residential specialists and have passed a difficult state exam. Be sure the appraiser has at least a four-year college degree from a good university and has had at least five years' residential appraisal experience in your market.

Ask your bank which appraiser they would recommend. By doing this, you can choose an appraiser who is reputable and qualified. You are also assured that the appraisal you pay for will be able to be used for the purposes of the loan.

Ask the appraiser about their turn-around time and request a list of lenders they are approved with. Each lender has a list of approved appraisers. Usually that means the appraiser's background, education and references have already been scrutinized and the bank has had some good experience working with that appraiser.

Things to Do

☐ Decide how you will approach estimating the value of your prospective home. Remember that your offer should be based on *your* assessment of market value, not the seller's list price.

☐ If you plan on using a CMA, ask your real estate agent about that service.

☐ If you plan on using an appraisal, start to collect information now on state-certified residential real estate appraisers. Order the real estate appraisal report before an offer or contract is presented to the seller. Use the appraisal for contract negotiations if necessary. Check with your lender to make sure the appraisal can be used for the loan associated with the purchase.

Step 8

Doing the Deal

Assuming that you have a good idea of your prospective home's market value, you should now know how to structure an offer that protects your best interests. Negotiating the contract for sale and going through the inspection process can be intimidating, but when you have a team of experts working for you, it takes the guesswork out of the deal. In this chapter we'll explain how to make a smart offer, what should be included in the sales contract and why a home inspection is important.

Making a Smart Offer

An offer involves much more than just suggesting a sales price. It's impossible to make an intelligent offer without spelling out *all* of the terms of the deal. An initial offer should always be made in writing and be presented in person by your real estate agent. In the interest of time, it's acceptable for counteroffers to be presented verbally or via fax. Upon acceptance, however, all parties must sign the contract and initial changes to make it binding. All contracts must be in writing and fully executed to be enforceable.

Your real estate agent will be a tremendous help to you during this process. Many times an agreement will be accepted immediately if the offer is presented in the right way and the terms of the contract are fair. There's a certain technique in making a smart offer.

Initially, you should gain as much information about the property as possible. You should also know of any additional costs you may be responsible for. Make sure you know what the exact property taxes are on the property. Are water, trash collection and sewer billed separately by local authorities? What are pool maintenance, electric and cable television costs? What are the monthly costs of the homeowners or condo association? Make sure you know all of these figures before making an offer, since they affect how much you'll spend on the home.

Insist on viewing the property disclosure statement. In this form, the seller discloses any known material defects or problems associated with the property. Past problems called *stigmas*, such as a murder on the premises, may not have to be disclosed by the seller, depending on state law. Most states do require the seller to provide a buyer with such disclosures, and in many states, it must be in writing. (See appendix for sample Real Estate Seller Disclosure Statement.)

Next, understand what the property is really worth. *Remember that the contract sales price amount should be based on your estimate of market value, not the seller's asking price.* You'll have to get an appraisal before a lender will approve your loan, anyway, so you will not lose anything by taking care of this step early. If you decide not to get an appraisal at this stage, make sure your real estate agent does a Comparative Market Analysis (CMA) of the property for you.

The price offered doesn't have to match the CMA or the appraised value exactly, especially if you feel the owner is desperate to sell. We suggest the *initial* offer should be at least 10 percent below your estimate of value. Offer an even lower amount if there is strong evidence of seller desperation. In fact, your initial offer should be as low as possible, without being unreasonable. If you insult or anger the seller with an offer that is too low, your chances of lowering the list price are slim. But, if you keep the seller negotiating, you still have a shot at making a good deal.

If the seller's asking price is low, great! Make an offer close to or matching this price and be happy to buy a home under market value. Do not feel that, because you did not bargain the price down, you did not get a good deal. You may have just found a home that was priced low and a good value.

The seller should not see the appraisal or C.M.A. unless absolutely necessary, but if the asking price is high, the hard data of comparable sales will offer a way to back up your offer and give you a lot more control over the process. Although your real estate agent should not advise you on how much specifically to offer, he or she can give you an idea of a property's market value and guide you through negotiations.

Before you make the initial offer, make up your mind in advance how much you want to pay for the property. Don't go beyond this price. If you are at a point where the sellers refuse to budge, it's better to walk away from a deal than to pay more than you feel the home is worth. Inevitably, negotiations will concentrate on price. This is when it is especially important to have an agent with appraisal experience on your side. It is difficult to argue with someone who really knows about value.

At the time the contract is presented, a cash deposit of one to five percent of the sales price is usually required. This money is also called a binder deposit, an *earnest money deposit* or an *escrow deposit,* and is put into what is called an *escrow account.* This money is an assurance to the seller that you are negotiating in good faith.

Along with this contract, you may include a letter of pre-qualification or pre-approval from a bank, just to show the seller that you can afford this price. Many smart agents also include some recent sales and listings of homes in the neighborhood that are lower in price than the subject property. This will aid in the acceptance of the offer. Make the seller aware that you know the market and you know your options. Theirs is not the only house for sale, and it may even be priced too high.

Once you make the initial offer, the seller must accept, reject or make changes to the offer within a specified time. The seller's agent is required to present all offers to the seller as soon as possible. If the seller does not respond in time, the entire contract technically becomes null and void. The buyer may want to make another offer with a new contract. If the first offer is rejected, your deposit may be recovered.

Your agent probably will be doing most of the negotiating for you, although it's up to you to set the price and terms on each offer and counteroffer. Again, no real estate agent should ever suggest to his client what specific price to offer on a property. An agent should offer only an estimate of market value and give his buyer/client as much information as possible regarding the seller's level of motivation or reasons for selling. An agent may also suggest strategies for negotiating and ideas on what to include in the contract, such as personal property or a home warranty.

There are various techniques and styles of negotiating. Some are friendly, while some are more confrontational. If sales price is an issue, try to find other areas of agreement. Closing dates, repairs, escrow amounts and closing costs are areas within a contract that can be negotiated. Sellers will be more likely to negotiate price if all other terms are agreeable. They've also invested more time in negotiations, so they'll be more inclined to reach for agreement rather than having to do it all over again with another party.

An attorney, a title company or the real estate agent may manage the escrow account. The money is typically kept in a non-interest bearing escrow account, but the two parties involved can decide what type of account they would like to use. This money will be ultimately contributed towards paying down the sales price of the home. If the offer is accepted, but the buyer defaults or decides not to go through with the sale, this deposit may be kept by the seller.

There are some ways to escape or back out of a contract legally without defaulting or forfeiting the deposit. The most common reasons a sale does not close are:

- Failure to receive financing.

- The property is not in satisfactory condition, according to home inspections, the cost of repairs exceed the limit stipulated in the contract, and the seller refuses to pay for the repairs.

- Title to the property contains defects and is not marketable, according to a title search.

Escape clauses regarding the above items are built into most sales contracts. Many standard contracts favor sellers and protect their best interests. Structuring a contract with additional escape clauses and other items that benefit the buyer is extremely smart.

When buying a new home and dealing with builders or developers, keep in mind that the possibilities of negotiating with them may be limited. Buying from a builder means you are dealing with a preset price that may be nonnegotiable. Prices are set on an a-la-carte basis according to the selected plans and specs of the home. Contracts used are constructed in a different way, and may include many addenda pertaining to special features.

Now let's talk about the particulars of a sales contract.

The Contract: Breaking Down the Parts

Although there are many variations, a typical residential sales contract usually consists of these sections:

- Description of the buyer, seller and property involved

- Purchase price

- Time for acceptance of offer

- Financing

- Title evidence

- Closing date

- Restrictions, occupancy, disclosures, clauses, assignability or other provisions

- Repairs, property condition or inspections

- Standards for real estate transactions and other miscellaneous items

- Broker detail

- Addenda

- Acceptance / Signatures

(See appendix for Contract for Sale and Purchase used by the Florida Association of Realtors and the Florida Bar.)

The buyer, not the seller, should have the sales contract prepared. Agents who work for the seller may want to prepare the contract, but do not allow this. Get the upper hand from the start by working with a contract prepared by you and those who are protecting your best interests. Know what is most important to you within the contract, so that as negotiations progress, items of lesser importance to you can be changed or omitted first. Don't let a relatively minor item be a deal breaker.

Ask your real estate agent for a preprinted sales contract form. Familiarize yourself with it and ask questions if you do not understand something. Most buyers use an attorney or their agent to help prepare a contract for them. Your attorney may use a different contract format from the one real estate agents use. In most states, the use of an attorney is not mandatory and is entirely up to you. As a general rule, an attorney should always be involved on any deal that is out of the ordinary, problematic or complex, or when the seller uses an attorney to change or add to the contract.

Consider the closing date carefully and think about how it will affect your life at the time of the move. You may need to think about when your lease is up or how long it may take to sell your current home. Make sure the date works best for you.

Obviously you must agree on the sales price. However, there are many other items on the contract that can affect your bottom line price. Appliances and other personal property to be left with the home, and what portion of the closing costs and home repairs the seller will pay will also affect your costs.

Title of the home must be clear of defects such as liens and encumbrances that may affect your ability to take ownership of the property. While this is usually a seller's expense, a title search and title insurance can be paid for by either party.

The contract should say that your deposit would be refunded if the sale were canceled due to financing problems. You can even specify that the sale can be canceled if you cannot get financing at an agreeable interest rate. You can make additions or changes to the sales contract, but the seller must agree to every change you make.

If there are any environmental concerns, you can negotiate who is responsible for any required testing or cleanup. You can also negotiate how expenses related to the property, such as taxes, utility bills and condominium fees, are to be divided on the closing date. You should be responsible only for the portion of these expenses owed after the date of sale. You can also negotiate settlement costs. Many costs are prorated, or divided proportionately, as of the date of closing.

A contingency, or an item that needs to be in place in order for the sale to occur, is important for a buyer to include in a contract. For example, you may want your purchase to be contingent upon selling your current residence at a minimum price by a specified date.

Included in the contract should be the right to cancel if you are not satisfied with the home inspection. Many contracts put limits on this; some may not include this provision at all. This is an important item, and can be spelled out in detail on an addendum page. Make this your number-one escape provision and negotiating chip. Anything found negative on the inspection report can be used to negotiate for a lower selling price or the seller will need to make repairs.

Many sellers include a home warranty as part of the listing. If they don't, you may ask for one as a part of the deal. This is an insurance policy that covers necessary repairs to the home usually for one year after the purchase. These policies vary widely, based on what systems of the home are covered and how much of the cost to repair is paid. For example, some policies don't cover pools and may require the homeowner to pay a high deductible to the contractor for each repair visit. Such a policy can be a good way of protecting yourself from a bad home inspection.

The Home Inspection: The Seller's Problems, Not Yours

It's imperative that you have your prospective home inspected. This is usually scheduled within ten days of the effective date of the contract. Don't make the mistake of skipping this step. An inspection will determine the condition of every major component and system of the home. The buyer, not the seller, should hire the inspector. This ensures that the inspector is working to protect the buyer's best interests.

Be present during the entire inspection. This will usually take from two to four hours or more, depending on the condition, type and size of the property. The inspector may not like being followed around during the inspection, but you will not only make sure the inspector is doing his or her job, you will also really learn the house and fully understand the inspection report in the process.

Usually your agent can refer you to a reputable inspector, but if you want to investigate inspectors on your own, here are some things to be aware of:

✔ Find out what is covered in the inspection and what is not. For example, some inspectors do not cover pools.

✔ Investigate the inspector's qualifications and references.

✔ Get an estimate of how much the inspection will cost. Usually inspection fees are similar to appraisal fees, depending on the property. The fees will vary, however, based on the size and structure of the property.

✔ Check to see if the inspector is licensed and insured.

✔ Get a blank copy of the inspector's report. Make sure it is not just a checklist or a short form. You should have a full, narrative report with detailed notes on the home and the problems that are found. Many times you can receive a copy of the completed report once the inspection is completed, since many inspectors are now armed with laptop computers and printers brought on-site.

The inspector should investigate every physical aspect of the property. An inspection should detail a property's type, age, remaining life, functional utility and condition. The structure, the roof, the electric, heating and cooling, plumbing, appliances, attic, windows and pool/spa should be examined.

Problems with the structure, foundation and roof are expensive and often cause buyers to back out of a contract. Make sure that the roof doesn't have advanced wear because replacing a roof could cost you thousands of dollars. If resurfacing is necessary, negotiate this with the seller. Inadequate insulation and ventilation can cause increased wear on the roof deck structure. This could cause expense later on in replacing the roofing shingles and roof deck and, if it's bad enough, the roof rafters will have to be replaced.

The inspector will look for bulges, deflections and other irregularities in the roof, exterior wall framing, interior framing or cracks in the foundation wall. These items could be symptoms of poor structural design, poor construction techniques, improper structural alteration, and water damage or termite damage. If there is a structural problem, it may be wise to negotiate the price of the home, based on an estimate of how much it will cost to repair the damage, or you may want to walk away from the deal altogether.

The inspector should also look at the paint on the walls if you are considering buying a home built before 1978. The walls could be covered with lead-based paint, which means you should be aware of lead-based paint laws and lead poisoning hazards. The inspector may suggest an X-ray evaluation to investigate if the paint surface has any lead content. The sales agent must give you a pamphlet that provides EPA-approved lead hazard information, plus the sales agent and seller must divulge what they know about the home's lead-based paint or lead-based hazards and give you any relevant information or reports. Additionally, the sales agent and the seller must attach a disclosure form to the agreement of sale that includes a Lead Warning Statement. All parties must sign an acknowledgment that the buyers have been notified.

Siding and windows should be inspected, since you don't want to be responsible for this later. The inspector should also make sure the land around the house is situated so water is diverted away from the home, to reduce the possibility of flooding.

The electrical system should be modern and up to current standards. Upgrading this system can be expensive. The inspector should check for potential problems, such as burned wiring, overloaded circuits, improper wiring connections, openings in the panel, home-installed wiring and aluminum wiring without the approved wiring connections. Older homes with knob-and-tube wiring may need to be completely rewired.

The inspector will look at the plumbing, checking for the condition and distribution of the pipes in the home. If there is plaster or wallboard that looks questionable, the inspector should have a moisture meter to evaluate any damage that might have been caused by water leaks. All fixtures and faucets should be operating properly and the bathtub and shower enclosures must be sound.

The heating and air-conditioning systems need to be checked to ensure that the furnace heat exchangers are working, the boilers are not leaking and the air-conditioner compressor is cooling properly. The heat distribution piping or ductwork also needs to be in good condition. Safety concerns, such as defective controls, emergency switches that do not work, evidence of past malfunctions, asbestos insulation and carbon monoxide emissions, must be checked out by your inspector. These are all items that you may insist on having fixed before you close on your new home.

If the home has been poorly maintained in general, there could be major problems that are not readily visible. If the home looks bad cosmetically, the condition of the less visible systems of the home could be worse. Be cautious of homes that have had extensive plumbing or electrical work, structural additions or renovations that were not professionally done. Proper codes or construction practices may not have been followed. Ask to see permits or plans if there is evidence of major renovation.

Have tests run on underground storage tanks or well-supplied drinking water. Checking for bacteria in your water source and radon gas in the air is also a good idea. All of these items can affect your health.

At the end of the inspection, you should receive a detailed written report that explains the condition of the home you are purchasing, including all positive and negative results. Know what specific repairs are needed, as well as how urgent the repairs are. Ask for an estimate of the repair costs, the proper course of corrective action or any possible alternatives to repairing an item. You should also know if there are any unsafe conditions or risks of hidden deterioration.

Once you receive your inspection report, your real estate agent can help you negotiate for the repairs you want completed. Be prepared to play a bit of hardball. Sellers understandably want to receive the most money they can out of the sale of their home and may not want to pay the costs of repairs. Decide which repairs cost the most and be concerned with those items. The inspector should be able to help estimate the cost of certain repairs, and this will help you decide which items can be overlooked. However, it may be necessary to get estimates from repairmen or contractors to make sure you aren't taking on more than you can handle. Your agent should be able to help arrange this for you.

Don't blow the deal over a minor cosmetic item that can be easily fixed. The seller does not necessarily have to fix everything. If you get too nit-picky with small ticket items, the seller may not agree to sell at all. Pick your battles carefully and consider the cost of repairs first and foremost.

Insist that licensed contractors do all of the repairs. Get the names of the repairmen and get a copy of their credentials to make sure a professional does the work. The seller's relatives may do a great job in their basement workshop, but you probably don't want them doing the electrical rewiring of your home. Make sure there is a stipulation about this in your contract.

Frequently buyers will have second thoughts or doubts about their purchase. This is called "buyer's remorse," and usually occurs from 24 hours to two weeks after the contract has been signed and accepted. Call your real estate agent and ask to see the home again. Chances are, seeing the house once more will calm your fears. You have spent a long time investigating and working with your agent, and it's likely that your anxiety is unfounded. If, after viewing the property, you want out of the contract, it's time to discuss your options with your agent.

Things to Do

- [ ] Decide who will prepare the sales contract — your real estate broker, attorney or both — and then put them to work. Do not attempt to do this on your own.

- [ ] Make sure to base your offer on your appraised value, include an escape provision regarding satisfactory property inspection, and include any contingencies necessary.

- [ ] Review the contract thoroughly.

- [ ] Use this contract as the vehicle for making the offer and have your real estate agent deliver the contract in person. Have the appraisal or CMA handy if needed for negotiations.

- [ ] Be available for communications at all times in the days to follow since your agent may have counteroffers ready for you to consider.

- [ ] After signing the final version of the sales contract, hire a good home inspector and be prepared to attend the inspection.

- [ ] After reviewing the inspection report, decide which items are important enough to address with the seller, and be prepared for another possible round of negotiations.

Step 9

Closing the Deal

You're almost there. You've survived the negotiations, inspections have been completed to your satisfaction, the sales contract has been finalized and executed, and necessary repairs are underway. Now it's time to buy homeowner's insurance and begin the easiest but most nerve-wracking part of the process. You have to prepare to close the deal, sign papers until your hand cramps and then hand over a huge check. The good news is that, after all this, you are given the keys to your new home. Let's look at the closing and what your financial and administrative responsibilities will be.

Homeowner's Insurance: "It'll Never Happen to Me" and Other Myths

Some items need to be concluded in preparation for closing. The lender will still be working to finalize your loan and will need to see the appraisal, termite and building inspection reports, and the final version of the sales contract. A survey may also be required depending on the property type. A title search has to be performed, but the seller usually handles this. You must also purchase homeowner's insurance (a.k.a. hazard insurance), which is required whenever a home is financed.

Basic homeowner's insurance covers major hazards to the home, but what is covered is something you need to investigate.

95

Insurance companies have been changing their policies lately, moving to offer a-la-carte coverage. Separate policies may need to be purchased for hurricanes, flood and even landslides. If you are in a flood zone, your lender will require a separate flood insurance policy. Even if your lender doesn't require it or if you're not in a flood zone, it still may be a good idea to purchase flood insurance.

When choosing a homeowner's policy, consider ones that package many kinds of insurance together. The least expensive and most basic policy is called HO-1 and provides reimbursement for common kinds of loss, such as fire, windstorm, glass breakage, theft, vandalism and liability. The broader, more expensive version, known as HO-2, adds items such as plumbing, heating and electrical systems. HO-3 is an all-risk version, and HO-6 is used for condominiums, townhouses and cooperatives. State regulations dictate the specific coverage in the various policies.

You can save on insurance by choosing a larger deductible. It's unlikely that you would want to deal with filing claims for losses of $250. Agreeing to handle a larger amount of money on any kind of loss on your own can cut premiums substantially. Insurance is used for catastrophic events. Look into the costs for different deductible levels. You should also make sure that the insurance company will pay the full replacement value of any item that is destroyed or damaged. For example, if your 20-year-old roof is destroyed, you should insist that a new roof be paid for. You should not be reimbursed for only the depreciated value of an older roof.

Another way to cut insurance costs is to allow one insurance company to cover all of your insurance needs. For example, many insurance companies that offer homeowner's insurance also offer car insurance. When you buy all types of insurance from one company, you may qualify for a lower rate or premium.

The policy needs to be purchased before final loan approval and, of course, closing. Like anything else, comparison-shop for insurance policies and ask your real estate agent for some names of good insurance professionals. Saving money here is important since this is a recurring cost that affects the size of your monthly payment. Remember that taxes and insurance are a part of your monthly mortgage payment, and the policy may be in place for the length of your ownership of the property.

Preparing for Closing:
Get Your Pen Ready

Final loan approval should occur soon after all documents are turned in. A title company, lawyer, bank, county courthouse, escrow service or real estate brokerage can handle the closing on real property. The title agent can now calculate all costs of closing and begin preparing the necessary documents.

You should be given a copy of the closing statement a day or two before closing, which will give you a chance to review all of your costs. A closing statement or HUD-1 settlement statement details all of the costs associated with the deal. It lists buyer's and seller's costs separately.

Carefully look for mistakes or surprise costs. Numbers can easily be corrected, even if you find something the day of closing. There are more mistakes on closing statements than most people realize. This may be due to simple math errors, sneaky small-print lending costs, or a communication breakdown within the huge number of service individuals involved in the deal. Your real estate agent can also help you look over this very important statement. (See appendix for a Sample Settlement Statement.)

A final walk-through of your home should always be performed. Your agent can join you to view the home the day of closing, or a day or two before closing, just to make sure all agreed-to repairs have been performed and the house hasn't been destroyed in any way. It's like checking a product one last time before actually paying.

The closing day may be scheduled before the closing date listed on the contract if both parties agree and all closing documents are ready. The seller may request to stay in the house a few days later than the closing date, if needed. Although this is not recommended, you can allow it if a proper addendum is prepared to cover the liability. You also should require adequate money to be held in escrow to cover yourself in case of foul play.

At the closing you will be required to bring proper identification and a money order or certified check for the down payment or escrow balance listed on the closing statement. Give yourself plenty of time to go to the bank.

Bring your personal checkbook for miscellaneous expenses that could arise. Sometimes the sellers will pre-sign documents and not attend closing if the closing date is not convenient, or if they were beat up a little in negotiations. This leaves you in attendance with the closing agent, and possibly a lender, mortgage broker, attorney, or your real estate agent.

Now, get your favorite pen ready. The closing agent will explain all papers to be signed.

The Costs of Closing

There are many costs associated with the closing on a new home. Here are some examples:

- Lender-required settlement costs (which may include private mortgage insurance)

- Statutory costs

- Third-party costs

- Miscellaneous costs

Lender-required settlement costs are items such as a new survey, appraisal and title insurance. Title insurance protects you from any forgeries, divorce claims, liens or encumbrances you may not be aware of. Remember that there is the lender's title insurance and the owner's title insurance. You should have owner's title insurance to protect yourself, which is a cost usually paid by the seller. The lender may also order and charge you for other settlement-related fees, such as loan processing, document preparation, credit report, underwriting, flood certification or an application fee.

If the lender will be paying taxes, hazard insurance and private mortgage insurance from an escrow account, you will probably have to pay two to three months' charges as a closing cost to pay for the account. Property taxes are prorated, with each party paying a proportionate share for their ownership period.

You may also be required to pay *Private Mortgage Insurance (PMI)* if you plan to put less than 20 percent down. Private Mortgage Insurance is a type of guarantee that helps to protect lenders against the costs of foreclosure. It enables lenders to accept lower down payments than they would normally by providing lenders the money that they would have received if the buyer had put down a larger down payment. Let's use an example.

Home buyer Steven puts down 20 percent for his home. He is unable to pay his mortgage payments and goes into foreclosure. The bank is somewhat protected from any costs they might incur because they already own 20 percent of the deal. However, let's say home buyer Craig puts down 10 percent for his home and was unable to make his mortgage payments. The bank does not have as large a chunk of the purchase price up front, which means they have the same costs, but not as much money to pay those costs. If Craig pays private mortgage insurance, the bank feels more comfortable lending him money because it means that there is less risk of losing money on the deal.

Mortgage insurance is just added protection for lenders, allowing them to loan money to people that they might not be able to otherwise.

PMI can be paid monthly with an initial monthly premium paid at closing and an equal renewal premium paid each month, or it can be paid annually with an initial premium paid at closing and a smaller renewal premium paid each month. It also can be paid as a single premium plan, which is a lump sum paid at closing that covers the insurance costs for a set number of years. In most cases, the lender will allow cancellation of mortgage insurance when the loan is paid down to 80 percent of the original property value.

Statutory costs are expenses that are paid to state and local agencies. These costs are required even if you pay cash for your home and are not taking out a mortgage. Transfer taxes and documentary stamps are examples of these costs. Some areas charge to transfer the title and deed from the seller to you. The county clerk charges fees to record the deed and the mortgage and to change the property tax billing. State and local fees vary, so you may have to pay some not listed here.

State or local taxes and condo or homeowners' association fees may also be due where applicable. These, too, are charged on a prorated basis. Depending on what time of year you close on the house, you may have to pay the seller back for costs they have prepaid.

Third-party costs are expenses paid to others, such as home inspectors, attorney's fees, homeowner's insurance, real estate agent's commissions and title search costs. The title search is done to ensure there are no problems such as liens or lawsuits that might keep you from taking possession of your home. This is done through a title company or an attorney.

Lenders usually require you to prepay the first year's premium for homeowner's insurance and bring proof of payment to closing. This means that, even if the house is destroyed, their investment will be safe. The real estate commission is another third-party cost, but the seller usually pays this expense. It is important to remember that even the commission is negotiable between the seller and the agent.

The up-front binder deposit you make at the time of the original offer and the remaining cash down payment you make at the closing will be credited against your expenses and the purchase price of the home. If additional inspections are required, such as water quality and radon tests, they may represent extra expenses. You must consider the cost of moving, as well as any money you may want to give to the seller for desired items not included in the purchase offer.

Miscellaneous costs can include additional costs of cleanup, radon mitigation procedures, house painting or appliance repair. To protect yourself from these added expenses, you should request that the seller set up an escrow account to cover any costs associated with these items. You may also insist that the seller pay for some repairs out of closing. Ask the seller's agent to provide the receipts from the repairs already performed. If something has not been repaired, or if you see items that are broken or missing, get reimbursed.

To save some closing costs, ask if each cost can be lessened, waived or handled in a different way that could be less expensive. You must ask for this to happen. Be aggressive! It could save you hundreds of dollars. For instance, instead of getting a new property survey done, see if the old one can be updated. You can save as much as 50 percent on that fee. If the seller is eager to sell, see if he or she will take over some of the closing costs.

Another item that can get expensive is the PMI insurance we mentioned earlier. If you can, bite the bullet and get that down payment to the 20 percent mark. Ask that rich uncle for the money, or cash in some mutual funds. If you do get a large sum of money from a relative or a friend, be prepared to produce a gift letter from that person along with a canceled check. Your lender or mortgage broker is likely to ask for it during the pre-approval process.

Request to review your closing documents, your loan papers, your abstract of title, your survey, and any other papers before you sit down to sign. These documents may be drawn up the day of closing, but do not feel pressure to sign anything you have not reviewed carefully. By requesting to see these documents before closing, you get an opportunity to read and understand what you will be signing.

Among these documents are the bond (note), which is the personal promise to pay the loan, and the mortgage, which is the financial lien against the property that allows the lender to foreclose if you default on the loan. You will have to live with the terms of these important legal documents for as long as you own the property. Make sure there are no hidden loopholes which may come back to cause problems later.

As with any other transaction we have discussed in this book, it is important to understand what you are signing. Ask questions, either to the title company, your real estate agent, or a real estate attorney. Any of these people can help you understand the complexities of the closing. Also ask about any of the fees discussed above. If you are being charged too much or are being asked to pay something you did not expect, it is your duty to find out why. Protect yourself by being as informed as possible before the closing and you will feel more in control of the process.

After all documents have been signed, you are then handed the keys to your new home!

Things to Do

☐ Prepare for closing by checking with your lender to make sure they have all the documents needed for final loan approval. The documents you are responsible for may include the appraisal, survey, termite and building inspection reports, and the final version of the sales contract.

☐ Buy all of the various types of homeowner's insurance needed and provide proof of this to the lender.

☐ Prepare for your move by packing, reserving a moving company, and contacting gas, cable, trash, electric, phone and water companies. More about the timeline of your move will be found in the next chapter.

☐ Get a copy of the closing statement a day or two before closing and carefully review all of your costs.

☐ Review any other documents to be signed at closing.

☐ Perform a final walk-through of the home a day or two before closing to check the condition and inventory of the home.

☐ At closing, bring proper identification and a money order or certified check for the down payment or balance due listed on the closing statement.

Step 10

Moving into and Improving Your New Home

Congratulations! You are now the owner of a home. You should have years of enjoyment making that house your own. Now it's moving time. Planning your move will help to make the task less burdensome, and we have some suggestions that will help ease your transition from home to home.

Once moved in, it's a natural reaction to start a million projects that will give the house your personal touch. However, it is important not to over-improve, as you will not get your money back when you go to resell your property. Along with suggestions for planning the timeline of your move, we will also investigate the financing and tax implications of improving your home and detail the improvements that will allow you to add to the value of your investment.

Before the Move: Methods for Keeping the Chaos to a Minimum

There are many items you can handle before moving that will make your life less chaotic. For example:

1. Fill out an IRS change of address form and change your address with the post office.
2. Notify important individuals of your new address, like friends, relatives, physicians, attorneys, stockbrokers and your dentist.

3. Inform your bank, credit card companies, insurance company, church, Department of Motor Vehicles, Social Security Administration, the voter registrar and any magazines you receive of your new address. Arrange for record transfers between schools, if necessary.

4. Gather moving supplies, such as boxes, tape and rope. Pack all nonessential items at this time.

5. Make travel arrangements, like airline, hotel or rental car reservations.

6. Call the chamber of commerce in your new area for a residential information packet of where to go for goods and services once you move.

7. If you are going to hire a moving company, reserve one in advance. If you are unsure what company you should entrust your belongings to, ask your real estate agent or local homeowners for some reputable names. Make sure the moving company is licensed, insured and has been in business for at least five years. You can do a check on moving companies by calling the Better Business Bureau, which will let you know if there are complaints against a particular moving company and how long it has been in business.

8. Ask for estimates from at least three moving companies. Also, be aware that a moving company will require cash or a certified check before they will unload the truck. Make sure you have a firm price, because if the moving company overcharges you may have little recourse. Ask for a cap on the price in writing.

9. Two weeks before the move, let the gas, electric, water, cable, and trash removal services know you are changing addresses. Also inform your pest control, landscaping and pool service providers that you will no longer need their services at your old home.

10. Call the phone company and get the telephone and all other services turned on at your new residence. You will need that phone to order pizza for the first couple of days until you get your house together!

11. Get your money back for any deposits made to the utility company or your landlord. Close any bank accounts or transfer any bank funds, if necessary. Return library books and retrieve dry cleaning.

12. Confirm any travel reservations to ensure your move is not held up with unnecessary delays. Make travel arrangements for pets, and remind friends and relatives who will be helping with your move to be ready. Make plans for young children to be cared for the day of the move. Fill prescriptions and medications needed for the next few weeks. Have your cars serviced and gas tanks filled.

13. Finally, before you move out of your old home, you must first do some extensive spring-cleaning. Consider having a yard sale to get rid of those items you have not touched for years. You could use the extra cash to hire someone to help you move! Do not make the mistake of moving junk to your new home. It can become costly, since moving companies sometimes charge by the weight of the items to be moved.

Time to Saddle Up and Move 'Em Out!

On moving day, important items to keep on hand are boxes, bubble wrap, marking pens, a tape measure, furniture pads or old blankets, packing tape and scissors, money and credit cards. Make sure each box is labeled with the room to which it should be delivered in the new home to help alleviate confusion later. Some even find it helpful to take a Polaroid snapshot of each box's contents and tape it directly to the box. Don't forget to mark any fragile items so the movers will know to be careful with them or hire the moving company to pack for you.

Pack a bag of personal items you'll need during the move, like clothes, toiletries, medicine, maps, food and drinks. Keep it in an easy-to-find place when you pack. If you have children, pack a bag of games and activities for them for the trip. Also, do not forget to put all legal, medical, dental, veterinary, accounting and insurance records in a safe place. You are about to turn your life upside down – don't misplace these important items in the process of moving.

Save all of your moving receipts, since up to $3,000 of moving costs may be tax-deductible. You can deduct the cost of moving your household goods and possessions and the cost of travel (excluding meals) for yourself and your family from your old home to your new home. This only applies, however, for those people who have a new job and whose new job location is at least 50 miles farther from their old home. For example, if your work was ten miles from home, the new job location must be at least 60 miles from the previous residence. Check with your accountant or tax adviser to see what applies in your situation.

Be at the house when the movers arrive. If this is not possible, have someone you trust be at the home when they come, so an informed individual can answer questions. Have that person accompany the movers through the house as they inventory your belongings. Make sure an accurate description of each item is recorded on the inventory and make a final check to be sure you have left nothing behind. Don't forget to check the closets, drawers, cabinets and attic.

Don't leave the home until everything is loaded on the truck, and give the movers your address and clear directions to your new home. Give them phone numbers where you can be reached in the interim and make sure you get the driver's name. Leave your forwarding address and an extra set of keys with the new owners or reliable neighbors. Before leaving the house, turn down the water heater, set the thermostat at 60 degrees if heat is needed, or at 80 degrees if it's warm enough for air conditioning, and turn off the faucet and the lights. Finally, don't forget to remove trash and leave the house in broom-clean condition.

Smart Money Home Improvements: Projects for Resale Victory

So you've made it into your new home, you've finally gotten all of your belongings into the perfect places and given the place a good cleaning. After the dust has settled, you may start looking around to see what projects to tackle first. Your local hardware or home improvement store bill may start to skyrocket and you will soon feel the need to prioritize your projects. Do this by categorizing the projects, considering the ability of each to add to the value of your home. Think of the costs of the project compared to the return on investment or future value of the home after re-pairs.

If you are considering a major project but are unsure about its investment potential, you can again use an appraisal to help you with the decision. Appraisals can be written as if the home improvements are in place and finished. Using builder's plans and specs, the appraisal report can include all square footage numbers, building materials and extras that will be a part of the home in the future. This can be done with existing homes or homes that are not yet built. Using this future appraised value, you can compare the estimated cost of the project to the indicated market value listed in the report. If the cost of the project exceeds the future appraised value, you can change the project or not perform this work at all. This approach can save you thousands and prevent you from making unwise improvements.

Home improvements can be viewed on three levels:

Level 1: Repairs or Replacements. In this scenario, items are repaired, replaced or maintained only, and all money invested may add nothing to the value of the home beyond the appeal of a well-maintained home. This work may offer no tax benefit and is considered to be the basic cost of owning and maintaining a home. Work may include fixing gutters, mending leaks, patching the roof, replacing an air conditioning unit, repairing appliances, replacing broken window panes or resealing the driveway.

Level 2: Home Improvements for Dummies. In this scenario, the money invested on the improvement exceeds the value it adds to the property. Work being done to a residence may add some value to the home and may be seen as an improvement in the tax world, but will not be a smart investment. Appraisers refer to this as an *over-improvement*. Examples would be adding a major wing to a residence, creating the largest house on the block or changing your home into an atypical, unpopular style because of your own personal tastes or adding an enormous amount of upgrades and amenities to your home. These can be disastrous moves financially when it's time to resell the home.

Level 3: Smart Money Home Improvements. In this scenario, the money invested in the improvement is less than the value it adds to the property. These are improvements that can be seen as smart investments. Let's concentrate our discussion on this category of home improvement.

Updating kitchens and baths is the best home improvement investment you can make, given the value added and the expense necessary for the work. If the kitchen in your new home is a little dated, you can remodel it and expect the most return on your investment. Renovating existing bathrooms will also give you a similar return. This is possible because you don't have to create the structure of the rooms as they already exist. This may enable you to keep expenses down by updating with new, relatively inexpensive, highly visible and marketable items such as fixtures, appliances, and cabinets. These rooms also tend to be important and are used frequently in most households.

Landscaping is another home improvement that offers a great return on investment. For relatively little money, the cosmetic appeal of a great-looking yard and garden can offer tremendous marketability to a property. This is probably the first thing a potential buyer will notice when driving up to your property. Real estate professionals refer to "curb appeal" when marketing homes. A deck for the backyard also offers a good return by adding to the outdoor living space.

Other cosmetic renovations that require relatively little expense, like interior and exterior painting and repair or replacement of flooring, can really add value. Doing the work yourself can be even more cost-effective. For paint, use popular, neutral colors. Try adding crown molding to frequently used rooms. For flooring, many people today are using tile, hardwood or other durable, easy-to-clean materials, especially in high traffic areas. These materials are also great for those with allergies and they last longer than carpeting.

Other good projects to invest in are room additions that add to a home's functional utility. For example, adding bedrooms, bathrooms, or enlarging a master suite can be smart choices. Make sure that the added square footage also adds to the property's functional utility. Adding a family room or other living area may not be useful and add nothing to a home's marketability. Converting an attic, basement or garage into finished living area can offer a good return on investment because, as we mentioned before, the basic structure is already in place. It is also more valuable if it does not detract from the aesthetics of your home.

New windows and doors can improve the look of a house, so items such as French doors may be a plus and add to the marketability and appeal of the home. Fences, walkways and other high visibility site improvements can also be smart additions.

One item you should think hard about before adding is a swimming pool. Many people consider a swimming pool an unnecessary expense and hassle. The market may or may not place a demand on this item. Obviously, this depends on where you live. The pool section of the Miami, Florida, yellow pages is much larger than it is in the Fargo, North Dakota, phone book.

When improving your home, remember not to over-improve it. Do not turn your residence into the most valuable home on the block. If you want a bigger and better home, buy another one in a better neighborhood.

Financing and Tax Implications of Home Improvements

Today, home improvement projects are being financed mainly in two ways. The most popular way of financing home improvements is the *Home Equity Loan*, sometimes referred to as an *equity line of credit* or a *second mortgage*. The equity of your home is used as collateral to extend a line of credit, much like a credit card. It is also a great way of using the equity in your home to pay off high-interest, nondeductible credit card and other debt, or to finance anything from education to vacations.

The second way, preferred by some homeowners, is simply to refinance their first mortgage with a new home improvement loan. Usually a lender will base the new loan on an "as-completed" value of the home. In other words, the value of the home is estimated based on its future value when all home improvements are completed. An "as-completed" appraisal may be performed using builder's plans and specs as a basis for estimating this new market value. A final inspection may be required when all work is done. Not all lenders offer this financing option, but it is a great way to leverage the potential, future value of your home before any work or expense is incurred.

There can be great tax benefits in improving your home. The interest on the mortgages discussed above can be deductible, just like your original mortgage. The points are also deductible, but must be amortized over the life of the loan. Also, the amount spent on home improvements can be added to the tax cost basis of your home. The IRS allows homeowners to add the price of improvements to the original cost basis of their property to arrive at a figure called the *adjusted cost basis*. Increasing your home's cost basis can reduce your taxable resale profits and thus reduce your tax burden.

Things to Do

☐ Move into your new home by planning ahead and packing logically.

☐ Alert all the necessary service companies and individuals associated with your new and old residences.

☐ Have a housewarming party!

☐ When improving your house, select only those projects that offer a good return on your investment. Investigate home improvement financing options and don't over-improve your current residence. Instead, use the smart money tactics you've learned in this book to simply buy another home.

☐ Reap all of the benefits of owning real estate and realize the pride of ownership enjoyed by homeowners throughout the world.

Appendix

Appendix A
Uniform Residential Loan Application

Uniform Residential Loan Application

This application is designed to be completed by the applicant(s) with the lender's assistance. Applicants should complete this form as "Borrower" or "Co-Borrower," as applicable. Co-Borrower information must also be provided (and the appropriate box checked) when ☐ the income or assets of a person other than the "Borrower" (including the Borrower's spouse) will be used as a basis for loan qualification or ☐ the income or assets of the Borrower's spouse will not be used as a basis for loan qualification, but his or her liabilities must be considered because the Borrower resides in a community property state, the security property is located in a community property state, or the Borrower is relying on other property located in a community property state as a basis for repayment of the loan.

I. TYPE OF MORTGAGE AND TERMS OF LOAN

Mortgage Applied for:	☐ VA ☐ Conventional ☐ Other: ☐ FHA ☐ FmHA		Agency Case Number		Lender Case No.
Amount $	Interest Rate %	No. of Months	Amortization Type:	☐ Fixed Rate ☐ Other (explain): ☐ GPM ☐ ARM (type):	

II. PROPERTY INFORMATION AND PURPOSE OF LOAN

Subject Property Address (street, city, state, & zip code)	County	No. of Units

Legal Description of Subject Property (attach description if necessary)	Year Built

Purpose of Loan	☐ Purchase ☐ Construction ☐ Refinance ☐ Construction-Permanent	☐ Other (explain):	Property will be: ☐ Primary Residence ☐ Secondary Residence ☐ Investment

Complete this line if construction or construction-permanent loan.

Year Lot Acquired	Original Cost $	Amount Existing Liens $	(a) Present Value of Lot $	(b) Cost of Improvements $	Total (a + b) $

Complete this line if this is a refinance loan.

Year Acquired	Original Cost $	Amount Existing Liens $	Purpose of Refinance	Describe Improvements ☐ made ☐ to be made Cost: $	

Title will be held in what Name(s)	Manner in which Title will be held	Estate will be held in: ☐ Fee Simple ☐ Leasehold (show expiration date)

Source of Downpayment, Closing Costs and/or Payoff Funds (explain)		

III. BORROWER INFORMATION

Borrower	Co-Borrower
Borrower's Name (include Jr. or Sr. if applicable)	Co-Borrower's Name (include Jr. or Sr. if applicable)

Social Security Number	Home Phone (incl. area code)	Age	Yrs. School	Social Security Number	Home Phone (incl. area code)	Age	Yrs. School

☐ Married ☐ Unmarried (include single, divorced, widowed) ☐ Separated	Dependents (not listed by Co-Borrower) no.	ages	☐ Married ☐ Unmarried (include single, divorced, widowed) ☐ Separated	Dependents (not listed by Borrower) no.	ages

Present Address (street, city, state, zip code) ☐ Own ☐ Rent _____ No. Yrs.	Present Address (street, city, state, zip code) ☐ Own ☐ Rent _____ No. Yrs.
If Mailing Address is different from above, please list on page 4.	If Mailing Address is different from above, please list on page 4.

If residing at present address for less than two years, complete the following:

Former Address (street, city, state, zip code) ☐ Own ☐ Rent _____ No. Yrs.	Former Address (street, city, state, zip code) ☐ Own ☐ Rent _____ No. Yrs.
Former Address (street, city, state, zip code) ☐ Own ☐ Rent _____ No. Yrs.	Former Address (street, city, state, zip code) ☐ Own ☐ Rent _____ No. Yrs.

IV. EMPLOYMENT INFORMATION

Borrower			Co-Borrower		
Name & Address of Employer ☐ Self-Employed		Yrs. on this job	Name & Address of Employer ☐ Self-Employed		Yrs. on this job
		Yrs. employed in this line of work/profession			Yrs. employed in this line of work/profession
Position/Title/Type of Business	Business Phone (incl. area code)		Position/Title/Type of Business	Business Phone (incl. area code)	

If employed in current position for less than two years or if currently employed in more than one position, complete the following:

Name & Address of Employer ☐ Self-Employed	Dates (from-to)	Name & Address of Employer ☐ Self-Employed	Dates (from-to)
	Monthly income $		Monthly income $
Position/Title/Type of Business	Business Phone (incl. area code)	Position/Title/Type of Business	Business Phone (incl. area code)
Name & Address of Employer ☐ Self-Employed	Dates (from-to)	Name & Address of Employer ☐ Self-Employed	Dates (from-to)
	Monthly income $		Monthly income $
Position/Title/Type of Business	Business Phone (incl. area code)	Position/Title/Type of Business	Business Phone (incl. area code)

MARRIED APPLICANTS ARE HEREBY NOTIFIED THAT THEY ARE ENTITLED TO APPLY FOR A SEPARATE ACCOUNT.

Borrower's Initials X _____
Co-Borrower's Initials X _____

V. MONTHLY INCOME AND COMBINED HOUSING EXPENSE INFORMATION

Gross Monthly Income	Borrower	Co-Borrower	Total	Combined Monthly Housing Expense	Present	Proposed
Base Empl. Income*	$	$	$	Rent	$	
Overtime				First Mortgage (P & I)		$
Bonuses				Other Financing (P & I)		
Commissions				Hazard Insurance		
Dividends/Interest				Real Estate Taxes		
Net Rental Income				Mortgage Insurance		
Other (before completing, see the notice in "describe other income." below)				Homeowner Assn. Dues		
				Other:		
Total	$	$	$	Total	$	$

*Self Employed Borrower(s) may be required to provide additional documentation such as tax returns and financial statements.

Describe Other Income **Notice:** Alimony, child support, or separate maintenance income need not be revealed if the Borrower (B) or Co-Borrower (C) does not choose to have it considered for repaying this loan.

B/C		Monthly Amount
		$

VI. ASSETS AND LIABILITIES

This statement and any applicable supporting schedules may be completed jointly by both married and unmarried Co-Borrowers if their assets and liabilities are sufficiently joined so that the Statement can be meaningfully and fairly presented on a combined basis; otherwise separate Statements and Schedules are required. If the Co-Borrower section was completed about a spouse, this Statement and supporting schedules must be completed about that spouse also.

Completed ☐ Jointly ☐ Not Jointly

ASSETS	Cash or Market Value	Liabilities and Pledged Assets. List the creditor's name, address and account number for all outstanding debts, including automobile loans, revolving charge accounts, real estate loans, alimony, child support, stock pledges, etc. Use continuation sheet if necessary. Indicate by (*) those liabilities which will be satisfied upon sale of real estate owned or upon refinancing of the subject property.		
Description		LIABILITIES	Monthly Payt. & Mos. Left to Pay	Unpaid Balance
Cash deposit toward purchase held by:	$	Name and address of Company	$ Payt./Mos.	$
List checking and savings accounts below				
Name and address of Bank, S&L, or Credit Union				
		Acct. no.		
		Name and address of Company	$ Payt./Mos.	$
Acct. no.	$			
Name and address of Bank, S&L, or Credit Union				
		Acct. no.		
		Name and address of Company	$ Payt./Mos.	$
Acct. no.	$			
Name and address of Bank, S&L, or Credit Union				
		Acct. no.		
		Name and address of Company	$ Payt./Mos.	$
Acct. no.	$			
Name and address of Bank, S&L, or Credit Union				
		Acct. no.		
		Name and address of Company	$ Payt./Mos.	$
Acct. no.	$			
Stocks & Bonds (Company name/number & description)	$			
		Acct. no.		
		Name and address of Company	$ Payt./Mos.	$
Life insurance net cash value				
Face amount: $				
Subtotal Liquid Assets	$			
Real estate owned (enter market value from schedule of real estate owned)	$	Acct. no.		
Vested interest in retirement fund	$	Name and address of Company	$ Payt./Mos.	$
Net worth of business(es) owned (attach financial statement)	$			
Automobiles owned (make and year)	$			
		Acct. no.		
Other Assets (itemize)	$	Alimony/Child Support/Separate Maintenance Payments Owed to:	$	
		Job Related Expense (child care, union dues, etc.)	$	
		Total Monthly Payments	$	
Total Assets a.	$	Net Worth (a minus b) ▶		Total Liabilities b.	$

Borrower's Initials X _____
Co-Borrower's Initials X _____

N34020

VI. ASSETS AND LIABILITIES (cont.)

Schedule of Real Estate Owned (If additional properties are owned, use continuation sheet.)

Property Address (enter S if sold, PS if pending sale or R if rental being held for income) ▼	Type of Property	Present Market Value	Amount of Mortgages & Liens	Gross Rental Income	Mortgage Payments	Insurance, Maintenance, Taxes & Misc.	Net Rental Income
		$	$	$	$	$	$
Totals		$	$	$	$	$	$

List any additional names under which credit has previously been received and indicate appropriate creditor name(s) and account number(s):

Alternate Name	Creditor Name	Account Number

VII. DETAILS OF TRANSACTION

a. Purchase price	$
b. Alterations, improvements, repairs	
c. Land (if acquired separately)	
d. Refinance (incl. debts to be paid off)	
e. Estimated prepaid items	
f. Estimated closing costs	
g. PMI, MIP, Funding Fee	
h. Discount (if Borrower will pay)	
i. Total costs (add items a through h)	
j. Subordinate financing	
k. Borrower's closing costs paid by Seller	
l. Other Credits (explain)	
m. Loan amount (exclude PMI, MIP, Funding Fees financed)	
n. PMI, MIP, Funding Fee financed	
o. Loan amount (add m & n)	
p. Cash from/to Borrower (subtract j, k, l, and o from i)	

VIII. DECLARATIONS

If you answer "yes" to any questions a through i, please use continuation sheet for explanation.

	Borrower Yes	Borrower No	Co-Borrower Yes	Co-Borrower No
a. Are there any outstanding judgments against you?	☐	☐	☐	☐
b. Have you been declared bankrupt within the past 10 years?	☐	☐	☐	☐
c. Have you had property foreclosed upon or given title or deed in lieu thereof in the last 7 years?	☐	☐	☐	☐
d. Are you a party to a law suit?	☐	☐	☐	☐
e. Have you directly or indirectly been obligated on any loan which resulted in foreclosure, transfer of title in lieu of foreclosure, or judgment? (This would include such loans as home mortgage loans, SBA loans, home improvement loans, educational loans, manufactured (mobile) home loans, any mortgage, financial obligation, bond, or loan guarantee. If "Yes," provide details, including date, name and address of Lender, FHA or VA case number, if any, and reasons for action.)	☐	☐	☐	☐
f. Are you presently delinquent or in default on any Federal debt or any other loan, mortgage, financial obligation, bond or loan guarantee? If "Yes," give details as described in the preceding question.	☐	☐	☐	☐
g. Are you obligated to pay alimony, child support, or separate maintenance?	☐	☐	☐	☐
h. Is any part of the down payment borrowed?	☐	☐	☐	☐
i. Are you a co-maker or endorser on a note?	☐	☐	☐	☐
j. Are you a U.S. citizen?	☐	☐	☐	☐
k. Are you a permanent resident alien? # _____	☐	☐	☐	☐
l. Do you intend to occupy the property as your primary residence? If "Yes," complete question m below.	☐	☐	☐	☐
m. Have you had an ownership interest in a property in the last three years? (1) What type of property did you own—principal residence (PR), second home (SH), or investment property (IP)? (2) How did you hold title to the home—solely by yourself (S), jointly with your spouse (SP), or jointly with another person (O)?	☐	☐	☐	☐

IX. ACKNOWLEDGEMENT AND AGREEMENT

The undersigned specifically acknowledge(s) and agree(s) that: (1) the loan requested by this application will be secured by a first mortgage or deed of trust on the property described herein; (2) the property will not be used for any illegal or prohibited purpose or use; (3) all statements made in this application are made for the purpose of obtaining the loan indicated herein; (4) occupancy of the property will be as indicated above; (5) verification or reverification of any information contained in the application may be made at any time by the Lender, its agents, successors and assigns, either directly or through a credit reporting agency, from any source named in this application, and the original copy of this application will be retained by the Lender, even if the loan is not approved; (6) the Lender, its agents, successors and assigns will rely on the information contained in the application and I/we have a continuing obligation to amend and/or supplement the information provided in this application if any of the material facts which I/we have represented herein should change prior to closing; (7) in the event my/our payments on the loan indicated in this application become delinquent, the Lender, its agents, successors and assigns, may, in addition to all their other rights and remedies, report my/our name(s) and account information to a credit reporting agency; (8) ownership of the loan may be transferred to successor or assign of the Lender without notice to me and/or the administration of the loan account may be transferred to an agent, successor or assign of the Lender with prior notice to me; (9) the Lender, its agents, successors and assigns make no representations or warranties, express or implied, to the Borrower(s) regarding the property, the condition of the property, or the value of the property.

Certification: I/We certify that the information provided in this application is true and correct as of the date set forth opposite my/our signature(s) on this application and acknowledge my/our understanding that any intentional or negligent misrepresentation(s) of the information contained in this application may result in civil liability and/or criminal penalties including, but not limited to, fine or imprisonment or both under the provisions of Title 18, United States Code, Section 1001, et seq. and liability for monetary damages to the Lender, its agents, successors and assigns, insurers and any other person who may suffer any loss due to reliance upon any misrepresentation which I/we have made on this application.

Borrower's Signature	Date	Co-Borrower's Signature	Date
X		X	

X. INFORMATION FOR GOVERNMENT MONITORING PURPOSES

The following information is requested by the Federal Government for certain types of loans relating to a dwelling, in order to monitor the Lender's compliance with equal credit opportunity, fair housing and home mortgage disclosure laws. You are not required to furnish this information, but are encouraged to do so. The law provides that a Lender may neither discriminate on the basis of this information, nor on whether you choose to furnish it. However, if you choose not to furnish it, and you apply in person, under Federal regulations this Lender is required to note race and sex on the basis of visual observation or surname. If you do not wish to furnish the above information, please check the box below.

BORROWER ☐ I do not wish to furnish this information.

Race/National Origin:
☐ American Indian or Alaskan Native ☐ Asian or Pacific Islander
☐ Black, not of Hispanic origin ☐ White, not of Hispanic origin
☐ Hispanic
☐ Other (specify)

Sex: ☐ Female ☐ Male

CO-BORROWER ☐ I do not wish to furnish this information.

Race/National Origin:
☐ American Indian or Alaskan Native ☐ Asian or Pacific Islander
☐ Black, not of Hispanic origin ☐ White, not of Hispanic origin
☐ Hispanic
☐ Other (specify)

Sex: ☐ Female ☐ Male

This application was taken by:	Interviewer's Name (print or type)	Name and Address of Interviewer's Employer
☐ face-to-face interview		☐ Bank of America
☐ mail	Interviewer's Signature / Date	☐ Loan Agent for Bank of America
☐ telephone	Interviewer's Phone Number (incl. area code)	☐ Other (specify) _____

Borrower's Initials X_____

Co-Borrower's Initials X_____

Continuation Sheet/Uniform Residential Loan Application

Use this continuation sheet if you need more space to complete the Residential Loan Application. Mark B for Borrower or C for Co-Borrower.	Borrower:	Agency Case Number:
	Co-Borrower:	Lender Case Number:

If Mailing Address is different from property address, please list below (street, city, state & zip code)

I/We fully understand that it is a Federal crime punishable by fine or imprisonment, or both, to knowingly make any false statements concerning any of the above facts as applicable under the provisions of Title 18, United States Code, Section 1001, et seq.

Borrower's Signature	Date	Co-Borrower's Signature	Date
X		X	

Borrower's Initials X
Co-Borrower's Initials X

N34040

Appendix B
Real Estate Seller Disclosure Statement

Property Address:_____ Inspection Date:_____
The following aspects of the above-referenced property have been personally inspected by the undersigned buyers and their condition noted accordingly on this form.

The disclosure statement concerns the real property situated in the city of _____ , county of _____ , State of California, described as _____ . This statement is a disclosure of the condition of the above described property in compliance with section 1102 of the Civil Code as of _____ , 19____ . It is not a warranty of any kind by the seller(s) or any agent(s) representing any principal(s) in this transaction, and is not a substitute for any inspections of warranties the principal(s) may wish to obtain.

Coordinate with Other Disclosure Forms: This Real Estate Transfer Statement is made pursuant to Section 1102 of the Civil Code. Other statutes require disclosures, depending upon the details of the particular real estate transaction (for example: special study zone and purchase-money liens on residential property).

Substituted Disclosures: The Seller disclosures have or will be in connection with this real estate transfer, and are intended to satisfy the disclosure obligations on this form, where the subject matter is the same: _____
_____
_____

Seller's Information: The Seller discloses the following information with the knowledge that even though this is not a warranty, prospective Buyers may rely on this information in deciding whether and on what terms to purchase the subject property. Seller hereby authorizes any agent(s) representing any principal(s) in this transaction to provide a copy of this statement to any person or entity in connection with any actual or anticipated sale of the property.

The following are representations made by the Seller(s) and are not the representations of the agent(s), if any. This information is a disclosure and is not intended to be part of any contract between the Buyer and Seller. Seller ☐ is ☐ is not occupying the property.

A. The subject property has the items checked below:

☐ Range	☐ Oven	☐ Microwave	☐ Dishwasher	☐ Trash Compactor
☐ Garbage Disposal	☐ W/D Hookups	☐ Window Screens	☐ Rain Gutters	☐ Burglar Alarm
☐ Smoke Detector(s)	☐ Fire Alarm	☐ TV Antenna	☐ Satellite Dish	☐ Intercom
☐ Central Heating	☐ Central Air Conditioning	☐ Evaporators Cooler(s)	☐ Wall/Wind Air Cond.	☐ Sprinklers
☐ Public Sewer System	☐ Septic Tank	☐ Sump Pump	☐ Water Softener	☐ Patio/Decking
☐ Built-in Barbecue	☐ Gazebo	☐ Sauna	☐ Pool	☐ Spa/Hot Tub
☐ Security Gate(s)	☐ Garage Door Opener(s)	☐ Attached Garage	☐ Not Attached Garage	☐ Carport
☐ Pool/Spa Heater—Gas	☐ Pool/Spa Heater—Solar	☐ Pool/Spa Heater—Electric	☐ Water Heater—Gas	☐ Water Heater—Solar
☐ Water Heater—Electric	☐ Water Supply—City	☐ Roof—Age_____	☐ Fireplace	

B. Are you (SELLER) aware of any significant defects/malfunctions: If yes, list/describe:
_____
_____
_____
_____

C. Are you (SELLER) aware of the following:

1. Substances, materials, or products that may be an environmental hazard such as, but not limited to, asbestos, formaldehyde, radon gas, lead-based paint, fuel or chemical storage tanks, and contaminated soil or water on the subject property. .... ☐ Yes ☐ No
2. Features of the property shared in common with adjoining landowners, such as walls, fences, and driveways, whose use or responsibility for maintenance may have an effect on the subject property............. ☐ Yes ☐ No
3. Any encroachments, easements, or similar matters that may affect your interest in the subject.............. ☐ Yes ☐ No
4. Room additions, structural modifications, or other alterations or repairs made without necessary permits. .... ☐ Yes ☐ No
5. Room additions, structural modifications, or other alterations or repairs not in compliance with building codes. .... ☐ Yes ☐ No
6. Landfill (compacted or otherwise) on the property or any portion thereof. .... ☐ Yes ☐ No
7. Any settling from any cause, or slippage, sliding, or other spoil problems. .... ☐ Yes ☐ No
8. Flooding, drainage, or grading problems. .... ☐ Yes ☐ No
9. Major damage to the property or any of the structures from fire, earthquake, floods, or landslides.............. ☐ Yes ☐ No
10. Any zoning violations, nonconforming uses, violations of "setback" requirements. .... ☐ Yes ☐ No
11. Neighborhood noise problems or other nuisances. .... ☐ Yes ☐ No
12. CC&R's or other deed restrictions or obligations. .... ☐ Yes ☐ No
13. Homeowners' Association that has any authority over the subject property. .... ☐ Yes ☐ No
14. Any "common area" (facilities such as pools, tennis courts, walkways, or other areas co-owned in undivided interest with others)... ☐ Yes ☐ No
15. Any notice of abatement or citations against the property. .... ☐ Yes ☐ No
16. Any lawsuits against the seller threatening to or affecting this real property. .... ☐ Yes ☐ No

Seller certifies that the information herein is true and correct to the best of the Seller's knowledge as of the date signed by the Seller.

Seller:_____ Date:_____

Appendix C
Exclusive Buyer Brokerage Agreement

Exclusive Buyer Brokerage Agreement
FLORIDA ASSOCIATION OF REALTORS®

1. PARTIES: _____ ("**Buyer**") grants
_____ ("**Broker**")
Real Estate Broker / *Office*
the exclusive right to work with and assist **Buyer** in locating and negotiating the acquisition of suitable real property as described below. The term "acquire" or "acquisition" includes any purchase, option, exchange, lease or other acquisition of an ownership or equity interest in real property.

2. **TERM:** This Agreement will begin on the _____ day of _____, 19___ and will terminate at 11:59 p.m. on the _____ day of _____, 19___ ("Termination Date"). However, if **Buyer** enters into an agreement to acquire property that is pending on the Termination Date, this Agreement will continue in effect until that transaction has closed or otherwise terminated.

3. **PROPERTY: Buyer** is interested in acquiring real property as follows or as otherwise acceptable to **Buyer** ("Property"):
   (a) Type of property: _____
   (b) Location: _____
   (c) Price range: $ _____ to $ _____
   ☐ **Buyer** has been ☐ pre-qualified ☐ pre-approved by _____
   for (amount and terms, if any)_____
   (d) Preferred terms and conditions:
   _____
   _____
   _____
   _____

4. **BROKER'S OBLIGATIONS:**
   (a) Broker Assistance. **Broker** will
      * use **Broker's** professional knowledge and skills;
      * assist **Buyer** in determining **Buyer's** financial capability and financing options;
      * discuss property requirements and assist **Buyer** in locating and viewing suitable properties;
      * assist **Buyer** to contract for property, monitor deadlines and close any resulting transaction;
      * cooperate with real estate licensees working with the seller, if any, to effect a transaction. **Buyer** understands that even if **Broker** is compensated by a seller or a real estate licensee who is working with a seller, such compensation does not compromise **Broker's** duties to **Buyer**.
   (b) Other Buyers. **Buyer** understands that **Broker** may work with other prospective buyers who want to acquire the same property as **Buyer**. If **Broker** submits offers by competing buyers, **Broker** will notify **Buyer** that a competing offer has been made, but will not disclose any of the offer's material terms or conditions. **Buyer** agrees that **Broker** may make competing buyers aware of the existence of any offer **Buyer** makes, so long as **Broker** does not reveal any material terms or conditions of the offer without **Buyer's** prior written consent.
   (c) Fair Housing. **Broker** adheres to the principles expressed in the Fair Housing Act and will not participate in any act that unlawfully discriminates on the basis of race, color, religion, sex, handicap, familial status, country of national origin or any other category protected under federal, state or local law.
   (d) Service Providers. **Broker** does not warrant or guarantee products or services provided by any third party whom **Broker**, at **Buyer's** request, refers or recommends to **Buyer** in connection with property acquisition.
   (e) Brokerage Relationship. **Buyer** acknowledges that this agreement does not create an agency or transaction brokerage relationship with **Broker**; however, **Buyer** and **Broker** may create such a relationship by separate document.

5. **BUYER'S OBLIGATIONS: Buyer** agrees to cooperate with **Broker** in accomplishing the objectives of this Agreement, including:
   (a) Conducting all negotiations and efforts to locate suitable property only through **Broker** and referring to **Broker** all inquiries of any kind from real estate licensees, property owners or any other source. If **Buyer** contacts or is contacted by a seller or a real estate licensee who is working with a seller or views a property unaccompanied by **Broker**, **Buyer** will, at first opportunity, advise the seller or real estate licensee that **Buyer** is working with and represented exclusively by **Broker**.
   (b) Providing **Broker** with accurate personal and financial information requested by **Broker** in connection with ensuring **Buyer's** ability to acquire property. **Buyer** authorizes **Broker** to run a credit check to verify **Buyer's** credit information.
   (c) Being available to meet with **Broker** at reasonable times for consultations and to view properties.
   (d) Indemnifying and holding **Broker** harmless from and against all losses, damages, costs and expenses of any kind, including attorney's fees, and from liability to any person, that **Broker** incurs because of acting on **Buyer's** behalf.
   (e) Not asking or expecting to restrict the acquisition of a property according to race, color, religion, sex, handicap, familial status, country of national origin or any other category protected under federal, state or local law.
   (f) Consulting an appropriate professional for legal, tax, environmental, engineering, foreign reporting requirements and other specialized advice.

6. **RETAINER:** Upon final execution of this Agreement, **Buyer** will pay to **Broker** a non-refundable retainer fee of $ _____ for **Broker's** services ("Retainer"). This fee is not refundable and ☐ will ☐ will not be credited to **Buyer** if compensation is earned by **Broker** as specified in this Agreement.

7. COMPENSATION: Broker's compensation is earned when, during the term of this Agreement or any renewal or extension, **Buyer** or any person acting for or on behalf of **Buyer** contracts to acquire real property as specified in this Agreement. **Buyer** will be responsible for paying **Broker** the amount specified below plus any applicable taxes but will be credited with any amount which **Broker** receives from a seller or a real estate licensee who is working with a seller.

(a) **Purchase or exchange:** $ _____ or _____ % (select only one) of the total purchase price or other consideration for the acquired property, to be paid at closing.

(b) **Lease:** $ _____ or _____ % (select only one) of the gross lease value, to be paid when **Buyer** enters into the lease. If **Buyer** enters into a lease-purchase agreement, the amount of the leasing fee which **Broker** receives will be credited with any amount which **Broker** receives will be credited toward the amount due **Broker** for the purchase.

(c) **Option: Broker** will be paid $ _____ or _____ % of the option amount (select only one), to be paid when **Buyer** enters into the option agreement. If **Buyer** enters into a lease with option to purchase, **Broker** will be compensated for both the lease and the option. If **Buyer** subsequently exercises the option, the amounts received by **Broker** for the lease and option will be credited toward the amount due **Broker** for the purchase.

(d) **Other: Broker** will be compensated for all other types of acquisitions as if such acquisition were a purchase or exchange.

(e) **Buyer Default: Buyer** will pay **Broker's** compensation immediately upon **Buyer's** default on any contract to acquire property.

8. PROTECTION PERIOD: Buyer will pay **Broker's** compensation if, within _____ days after Termination Date, **Buyer** contracts to acquire any property which was called to **Buyer's** attention by **Broker** or any other person or found by **Buyer** during the term of this Agreement. **Buyer's** obligation to pay **Broker's** fee ceases upon **Buyer** entering into a good faith exclusive buyer brokerage agreement with another broker after Termination Date.

9. EARLY TERMINATION: Buyer may terminate this Agreement at any time by written notice to **Broker** but will remain responsible for paying **Broker's** compensation if, from the early termination date to Termination Date plus Protection Period, if applicable, **Buyer** contracts to acquire any property which, prior to the early termination date, was found by **Buyer** or called to **Buyer's** attention by **Broker** or any other person. **Broker** may terminate this Agreement at any time by written notice to **Buyer**, in which event **Buyer** will be released from all further obligations under this Agreement.

10. DISPUTE RESOLUTION: Any unresolveable dispute between **Buyer** and **Broker** will be mediated. If a settlement is not reached in mediation, the matter will be submitted to binding arbitration in accordance with the rules of the American Arbitration Association or other mutually agreeable arbitrator.

11. ASSIGNMENT; PERSONS BOUND: Broker may assign this Agreement to another broker. This Agreement will bind and inure to **Broker's** and **Buyer's** heirs, personal representatives, successors and assigns.

12. RADON GAS: Radon is a naturally occurring radioactive gas that, when it has accumulated in a building in sufficient quantities, may present health risks to persons who are exposed to it over time. Levels of radon that exceed federal and state guidelines have been found in buildings in Florida. Additional information regarding radon and radon testing may be obtained from your county public health unit.

13. SPECIAL CLAUSES:

_____
_____
_____
_____
_____
_____
_____

14. ACKNOWLEDGMENT; MODIFICATIONS: Buyer has read this Agreement and understands its contents. This Agreement cannot be changed except by written agreement signed by both parties.

Date: _____ Buyer: _____ Tax ID No: _____

Address: _____

Zip: _____ Telephone: _____ Facsimile: _____

Date: _____ Buyer: _____ Tax ID No: _____

Address: _____

Zip: _____ Telephone: _____ Facsimile: _____

Date: _____ **Real Estate Associate:** _____

Date: _____ **Real Estate Broker:** _____

Appendix D
Uniform Residential Appraisal Report

SUBJECT

Property Address	City	State Zip Code
Legal Description		County
Assessor's Parcel No.	Tax Year R.E. Taxes $	Special Assessments $
Borrower	Current Owner	Occupant: ☐ Owner ☐ Tenant ☐ Vacant
Property rights appraised ☐ Fee Simple ☐ Leasehold	Project Type ☐ PUD ☐ Condominium (HUD/VA only)	HOA$ /Mo.
Neighborhood/Project Name	Map Reference	Census Tract
Sale Price $ Date of Sale	Description and $ amount of loan charges/concessions to be paid by seller	
Lender/Client	Address	
Appraiser	Address	

NEIGHBORHOOD

Location	☐ Urban	☐ Suburban	☐ Rural	**Predominant occupancy**	**Single family housing**	**Present land use %**	**Land use change**
Built up	☐ Over 75%	☐ 25–75%	☐ Under 25%		PRICE $(000) AGE (yrs)	One family	☐ Not likely ☐ Likely
Growth rate	☐ Rapid	☐ Stable	☐ Slow	☐ Owner	Low	2–4 family	☐ In process
Property values	☐ Increasing	☐ Stable	☐ Declining	☐ Tenant	High	Multi–family	To:
Demand/supply	☐ Shortage	☐ In balance	☐ Over supply	☐ Vacant (0–5%)	Predominant	Commercial	
Marketing time	☐ Under 3 mos.	☐ 3–6 mos.	☐ Over 6 mos.	☐ Vacant(over5%)			

Note: Race and the racial composition of the neighborhood are not appraisal factors.

Neighborhood boundaries and characteristics:

Factors that affect the marketability of the properties in the neighborhood (proximity to employment and amenities, employment stability, appeal to market, etc.):

Market conditions in the subject neighborhood (including support for the above conclusions related to the trend of property values, demand/supply, and marketing time — such as data on competitive properties for sale in the neighborhood, description of the prevalence of sales and financing concessions, etc):

PUD

Project Information for PUDs (If applicable) – – Is the developer/builder in control of the Home Owners' Association (HOA)?   ☐ Yes ☐ No

Approximate total number of units in the subject project   Approximate total number of units for sale in the subject project

Describe common elements and recreational facilities:

SITE

Dimensions		Topography
Site area Corner Lot ☐ Yes ☐ No		Size
Specific zoning classification and description		Shape
Zoning compliance ☐ Legal ☐ Legal nonconforming (Grandfathered use) ☐ Illegal ☐ No zoning		Drainage
Highest&best use as improved: ☐ Present use ☐ Other use (explain)		View
Utilities Public Other Off–site improvements Type Public Private		Landscaping
Electricity ☐ Street		Driveway Surface
Gas ☐ Curb/gutter		Apparent easements
Water ☐ Sidewalk		FEMA Special Flood Hazard ☐ Yes ☐ No
Sanitary sewer ☐ Street lights		FEMA Zone Map Date
Storm sewer ☐ Alley		FEMA Map No.

Comments (apparent adverse easements, encroachments, special assessments, slide areas, illegal or legal nonconforming zoning, use, etc.):

DESCRIPTION OF IMPROVEMENTS

GENERAL DESCRIPTION	EXTERIOR DESCRIPTION	FOUNDATION	BASEMENT	INSULATION
No. of Units	Foundation	Slab	Area Sq.Ft.	Roof ☐
No. of Stories	Exterior Walls	Crawl Space	% Finished	Ceiling ☐
Type (Det./Att.)	Roof Surface	Basement	Ceiling	Walls ☐
Design (Style)	Gutters & Dwnspts.	Sump Pump	Walls	Floor ☐
Existing/Proposed	Window Type	Dampness	Floor	None ☐
Age (Yrs.)	Storm/Screens	Settlement	Outside Entry	Unknown ☐
Effective Age (Yrs.)	Manufactured House	Infestation		

ROOMS	Foyer	Living	Dining	Kitchen	Den	Family Rm.	Rec.Rm.	Bedrooms	# Baths	Laundry	Other	Area Sq.Ft.
Basement												
Level 1												
Level 2												

Finished area above grade contains: Rooms;   Bedroom(s);   Bath(s);   Square Feet of Gross Living Area

SURFACES	Materials/Condition	HEATING		KITCHEN EQUIP.		ATTIC		AMENITIES		CAR STORAGE:	
Floors		Type		Refrigerator		None	☐	Fireplace(s) #		None	☐
Walls		Fuel		Range/Oven		Stairs	☐	Patio		Garage	# of Cars
Trim/Finish		Condition		Disposal		Drop Stair	☐	Deck		Attached	
Bath Floor		COOLING		Dishwasher		Scuttle	☐	Porch		Detached	
Bath Wainscot		Central		Fan/Hood		Floor	☐	Fence		Built–In	
Doors		Other		Microwave		Heated	☐	Pool		Carport	
		Condition		Washer/Dryer		Finished	☐			Driveway	

COMMENTS

Additional features (special energy efficient items, etc.):

Condition of the improvements, depreciation (physical, functional, and external), repairs needed, quality of construction, remodeling/additions, etc.:

Adverse environmental conditions (such as, but not limited to, hazardous wastes, toxic substances, etc.) present in the improvements, on the site, or in the immediate vicinity of the subject

File No. SAMPLE

COST APPROACH

ESTIMATED SITE VALUE = $ ________
ESTIMATED REPRODUCTION COST–NEW–OF IMPROVEMENTS:
Dwelling ________ Sq.Ft. @ $ ________ = $ ________
________ Sq.Ft. @ $ ________ = ________
________ = ________
Garage/Carport ________ Sq.Ft. @ $ ________ = ________
Total Estimated Cost New = $ ________
Less Physical | Functional | External
Depreciation ________ | ________ | ________ = $ ________
Depreciated Value of Improvements = $ ________
"As–is" Value of Site Improvements = $ ________
INDICATED VALUE BY COST APPROACH = $ ________

Comments on Cost Approach (such as, source of cost estimate, site value, square foot calculation and for HUD, VA and FmHA, the estimated remaining economic life of the property): ________

SALES COMPARISON ANALYSIS

ITEM	SUBJECT	COMPARABLE NO. 1		COMPARABLE NO. 2		COMPARABLE NO. 3	
Address							
Proximity to subject							
Sales Price	$	$		$		$	
Price/Gross Liv. Area	$ ⌀	$ ⌀		$ ⌀		$ ⌀	
Data and/or Verification Source							
VALUE ADJUSTMENTS	DESCRIPTION	DESCRIPTION	+(–)Adjustment	DESCRIPTION	+(–)Adjustment	DESCRIPTION	+(–)Adjustment
Sales or Financing Concessions							
Date of Sale/Time							
Location							
Leasehold/Fee Simple							
Site							
View							
Design and Appeal							
Quality of Construction							
Age							
Condition							
Above Grade Room Count	Total | Bdrms | Baths	Total | Bdrms | Baths		Total | Bdrms | Baths		Total | Bdrms | Baths	
Gross Living Area	Sq.Ft.	Sq.Ft.		Sq.Ft.		Sq.Ft.	
Basement & Finished Rooms Below Grade							
Functional Utility							
Heating/Cooling							
Energy Efficient Items							
Garage/Carport							
Porch, Patio, Deck, Fireplace(s), etc.							
Fence, Pool, etc.							
Net Adj.(total)		☐ + ☐ – $		☐ + ☐ – $		☐ + ☐ – $	
Adjusted Sales Price of Comparable		Net % Gross % $		Net % Gross % $		Net % Gross % $	

Comments on Sales Comparison (including the subject property's compatibility to the neighborhood, etc.): ________

ITEM	SUBJECT	COMPARABLE NO. 1	COMPARABLE NO. 2	COMPARABLE NO. 3
Date, Price and Data Source for prior sales within year of appraisal				

Analysis of any current agreement of sale, option, or listing of the subject property and analysis of any prior sales of subject and comparables within one year of the date of appraisal:

INDICATED VALUE BY SALES COMPARISON APPROACH . . . . $ ________
INDICATED VALUE BY INCOME APPROACH (If applicable) Estimated Market Rent $ ________ /Mo. x Gross Rent Multiplier ________ = $ ________

RECONCILIATION

This appraisal is made ☐ "as is" ☐ subject to the repairs, alterations, inspections or conditions listed below ☐ subject to completion per plans and specifications.
Conditions of Appraisal: ________

Final Reconciliation: ________

The purpose of this appraisal is to estimate the market value of the real property that is the subject of this report, based on the above conditions and the certification, contingent and limiting conditions, and market value definition that are stated in the attached Freddie Mac Form 439/Fannie Mae Form 1004B (Revised ________).
I (WE) ESTIMATE THE MARKET VALUE, AS DEFINED OF THE REAL PROPERTY THAT IS THE SUBJECT OF THIS REPORT, AS OF ________
(WHICH IS THE DATE OF INSPECTION AND THE EFFECTIVE DATE OF THIS REPORT) TO BE $ ________

APPRAISER	SUPERVISORY APPRAISER (If applicable)
SIGNATURE	SIGNATURE ☐ Did ☐ Did Not
NAME	NAME Inspect Property
DATE REPORT SIGNED	DATE REPORT SIGNED
STATE CERTIFICATION # STATE	STATE CERTIFICATION # STATE
OR STATE LICENSE # STATE	OR STATE LICENSE # STATE

F

Appendix E
Individual Condominum Unit Appraisal Report

SUBJECT

Property Address	City / State / Zip Code
Legal Description	County / Unit No.
Assessor's Parcel No.	Tax Year / R.E. Taxes $ / Special Assessments $
Project Name/Phase No.	Map Reference / Census Tract
Borrower	Current Owner / Occupant: Owner ☐ Tenant ☐ Vacant ☐

Property rights appraised ☐ Fee Simple ☐ Leasehold   Monthly Home Owners' Association Unit Charge $

Sales Price $ ___ Date of Sale ___ Description and $ amount of loan charges/concessions to be paid by seller ___

Lender/Client ___ Address ___

Appraiser ___ Address ___

NEIGHBORHOOD

Location	Urban ☐	Suburban ☐	Rural ☐	Predominant single family occupancy	Single family housing PRICE $(000) / AGE (yrs)	Predominant condominium occupancy	Condominium housing PRICE $(000) / AGE (yrs)
Built up	Over 75% ☐	25–75% ☐	Under 25% ☐	Owner	Low	Owner	Low
Growth rate	Rapid ☐	Stable ☐	Slow ☐	Tenant	High	Tenant	High
Property values	Increasing ☐	Stable ☐	Declining ☐	Vacant (0–5%)	Predominant	Vacant (0–5%)	Predominant
Demand/supply	Shortage ☐	In balance ☐	Over supply ☐	Vacant (over 5%)		Vacant (over 5%)	
Marketing time	Under 3 mos. ☐	3–6 mos. ☐	Over 6 mos. ☐				

Present land use %: One Family ___ , 2–4 Family ___ , Apartments ___ , Condominium ___ , Commercial ___ , Industrial ___ , Vacant ___ , Other ___

Land use change: ☐ Not likely ☐ Likely ☐ In process to ___

Note: Race and the racial composition of the neighborhood are not appraisal factors.

Neighborhood boundaries and characteristics: ___

Factors that affect the marketability of the properties in the neighborhood (proximity to employment and amenities, employment stability, appeal to market, etc.): ___

Market conditions in the subject neighborhood (including support for the above conclusions related to the trend of property values, demand/supply, and marketing time -- such as data on competitive properties for sale in the project and neighborhood, description of the prevalence of sales and financing concessions, etc.): ___

SITE

Specific zoning classification and description	Topography ___
Zoning compliance ☐ Legal ☐ Legal nonconforming (grandfathered use) ☐ Illegal ☐ No zoning	Size ___
Highest & best use as improved ☐ Present use ☐ Other use (explain)	Density ___

Utilities	Public	Other	Off–site Improvements	Type	Public	Private	
Electricity			Street				View ___
Gas			Curb/gutter				Drainage ___
Water			Sidewalk				Apparent easements ___
Sanitary sewer			Street lights				FEMA Special Flood Hazard Area ☐ Yes ☐ No
Storm sewer			Alley				FEMA Zone ___ Map Date ___
							FEMA Map No. ___

Comments (apparent adverse easements, encroachments, special assessments, slide areas, illegal or legal nonconforming zoning use, etc.): ___

PROJECT IMPROVEMENTS

No. of Stories	Exterior Walls	If Project Completed:	If Project Incomplete:	Subject Phase:
No. of Elevator(s)	Roof Surface	Total No. of Phases	Total No. of Planned Phases	Total No. of Units
Existing/Proposed	Total No. Parking	Total No. of Units	Total No. of Planned Units	Total No. of Units Completed
If conversion, orig. use	Ratio (spaces/units)	Total No. of Units for Sale	Total No. of Units for Sale	Total No. of Units for Sale
Date of Conversion	Type	Total No. of Units Sold	Total No. of Units Sold	Total No. of Units Sold
Age (Yrs.)	Guest Parking	Total No. of Units Rented	Total No. of Units Rented	Total No. of Units Rented
Effective Age (Yrs.)		Data Source	Data Source	Data Source

Project Type: ☐ Primary Residence ☐ Second Home or Recreational ☐ Row or Townhouse ☐ Garden ☐ Midrise ☐ Highrise ☐

Condition of the project, quality of construction, unit mix, appeal to market, etc.: ___

Are the heating and cooling for the individual units separately metered? ☐ Yes ☐ No If no, describe and comment on compatibility to other projects in market area and market acceptance: ___

Describe common elements and recreational facilities: ___

Are the common elements completed? ☐ Yes ☐ No   Is the Builder/Developer in control of the Home Owners' Association? ☐ Yes ☐ No

Are any common elements leased to or by the Home Owners' Association? ☐ Yes ☐ No   If yes, attach addendum describing rental terms and options.

SUBJECT UNIT

ROOMS	Foyer	Living	Dining	Kitchen	Den	Family Rm.	Rec. Rm.	Bedrooms	# Baths	Laundry	Other	Area Sq. Ft.
Basement												
Level 1												
Level 2												

Finished area **above** grade contains: ___ Rooms; ___ Bedroom(s); ___ Bath(s); ___ Square Feet of Gross Living Area For Unit

GENERAL DESCRIPTION	HEATING	KITCHEN EQUIP.	AMENITIES	CAR STORAGE	INSULATION
Floor No.	Type	Refrigerator	Fireplace(s) #	None	Roof
No. of Levels	Fuel	Range/Oven	Patio	Garage	Ceiling
INTERIOR Materials/Condition	Condition	Disposal	Balcony	No. of Cars	Walls
Flooring	COOLING	Dishwasher	Deck	Open	Floor
Walls	Central	Fan/Hood	Porch	No. of Cars	None
Bath Floor	Other	Microwave	Fence	Parking Space No.	Unknown
Bath Wainscot	Condition	Washer/Dryer		Assigned/Owned	

COMMENTS

Condition of the unit, depreciation, repairs needed, quality of construction, remodeling/modernization, additional features (special energy efficient items, etc.): ___

Adverse environmental conditions (such as, but not limited to, hazardous wastes, toxic substances, etc.) present in the improvements, on the site, or in the immediate vicinity of the subject property: ___

The Smart Money Guide to Buying a Home

PROJECT ANALYSIS

Unit Charge $ _____ per mo. x 12 = $ _____ per yr.   Annual Assessment charge per year/square feet of gross living area = $ _____

Is the project subject to ground rent? ☐ Yes ☐ No   If yes, $ _____ per year.

Utilities included in unit charge: ☐ None ☐ Heat ☐ Air Conditioning ☐ Electricity ☐ Gas ☐ Water ☐ Sewer

Note any fees, other than regular HOA charges, for use of facilities

Compared to other competitive projects of similar quality and design, the subject unit charge appears: ☐ High ☐ Typical ☐ Low

To properly maintain the project and provide the services anticipated, the budget appears: ☐ Adequate ☐ Inadequate ☐ Unknown

Management Group: ☐ Home Owners' Association ☐ Developer ☐ Management Agent (Identify)

Quality of management and its enforcement of Rules and Regulations based on general appearance of project appears: ☐ Adequate ☐ Inadequate

Special or unusual characteristics in the Condominium Documents or other information known to the appraiser that would affect marketability (if none, so state)

SALES COMPARISON ANALYSIS

ITEM	SUBJECT	COMPARABLE NO. 1		COMPARABLE NO. 2		COMPARABLE NO. 3	
Address, Unit #, and Project Name							
Proximity to Subject							
Sales Price	$	$		$		$	
Price/Gross Liv. Area	$	$		$		$	
Data and/or Verification Sources							
VALUE ADJUSTMENTS	DESCRIPTION	DESCRIPTION	+ (–) $ Adjustment	DESCRIPTION	+ (–) $ Adjustment	DESCRIPTION	+ (–) $ Adjustment
Sales or Financing Concessions							
Date of Sale/Time							
Location							
Leasehold/Fee Simple							
HOA Mo. Assessment							
Common Elements and Rec. Facilities							
Project Size/Type							
Floor Location							
View							
Design and Appeal							
Quality of Construction							
Age							
Condition							
Above Grade Room Count	Total Bdrms Baths	Total Bdrms Baths		Total Bdrms Baths		Total Bdrms Baths	
Gross Living Area	Sq. Ft.	Sq. Ft.		Sq. Ft.		Sq. Ft.	
Basement & Finished Rooms Below Grade							
Functional Utility							
Heating/Cooling							
Energy Efficient Items							
Car Storage							
Balcony, Patio, Fireplace(s), etc.							
Net Adj. (total)		☐ + ☐ – $		☐ + ☐ – $		☐ + ☐ – $	
Adjusted Sales Price of Comparable		$		$		$	

Comments on Sales Comparison (including the subject property's compatibility to other condominium units in the neighborhood, etc.): _____

ITEM	SUBJECT	COMPARABLE NO. 1	COMPARABLE NO. 2	COMPARABLE NO. 3
Data, Price and Data Source for prior sales within year of appraisal				

Analysis of any current agreement of sale, option, or listing of the subject property and analysis of any prior sales of subject and comparables within one year of the date of appraisal:

RECONCILIATION

INDICATED VALUE BY SALES COMPARISON APPROACH . . . . $ _____

INDICATED VALUE BY INCOME APPROACH (If Applicable) Estimated Market Rent $ _____ /Mo. x Gross Rent Multiplier _____ = $ _____

INDICATED VALUE BY COST APPROACH (Attach If Applicable) . . . . $ _____

This appraisal is made ☐ "as is" ☐ subject to the repairs, alterations, inspections, or conditions listed below ☐ subject to completion per plans and specifications.

Conditions of Appraisal: _____

Final Reconciliation: _____

The purpose of this appraisal is to estimate the market value of the real property that is the subject of this report, based on the above conditions and the certification, contingent and limiting conditions, and market value definition that are stated in the attached Freddie Mac Form 439/Fannie Mae Form 1004B (Revised _____).

I (WE) ESTIMATE THE MARKET VALUE, AS DEFINED, OF THE REAL PROPERTY THAT IS THE SUBJECT OF THIS REPORT, AS OF _____ (WHICH IS THE DATE OF INSPECTION AND THE EFFECTIVE DATE OF THIS REPORT) TO BE $ _____

APPRAISER: SUPERVISORY APPRAISER (ONLY IF REQUIRED):

Signature _____   Signature _____   ☐ Did ☐ Did Not Inspect Property

Name _____   Name _____

Date Report Signed _____   Date Report Signed _____

State Certification # _____ State _____   State Certification # _____ State _____

Or State License # _____ State _____   Or State License # _____ State _____

Appendix F
Small Residential Income Property Appraisal Report

SUBJECT

Property Address	City	State — Zip Code
Legal Description		County
Assessor's Parcel No.	Tax Year — R.E. Taxes $	Special Assessments $
Neighborhood or Project Name	Map Reference	Census Tract
Borrower — Current Owner	Occupant	Owner ☐ Tenant ☐ Vacant ☐
Property rights appraised ☐ Fee Simple ☐ Leasehold	Project Type ☐ PUD ☐ Condominium	HOA$ — /Mo.
Sales Price $ — Date of Sale	Description and $ amount of loan charges/concessions to be paid by seller	
Lender/Client — Address		
Appraiser — Address		

Location	Urban ☐	Suburban ☐	Rural ☐	Predominant Single Family Occupancy	Single family housing		Predominant 2–4 Family Occupancy	2–4 family housing	
					PRICE $(000)	AGE (yrs)		PRICE $(000)	AGE (yrs)
Built up	Over 75% ☐	25–75% ☐	Under 25% ☐	Single Family			2–4 Family		
Growth rate	Rapid ☐	Stable ☐	Slow ☐	Owner	Low		Owner	Low	
Property values	Increasing ☐	Stable ☐	Declining ☐	Tenant	High		Tenant	High	
Demand/supply	Shortage ☐	In balance ☐	Over supply ☐	Vacant (0–5%)	Predominant		Vacant (0–5%)	Predominant	
Marketing time	Under 3 mos. ☐	3–6 mos. ☐	Over 6 mos. ☐	Vacant (over 5%)			Vacant (over 5%)		

Typical 2–4 family bldg. Type — No. stories — No. units — Age — yrs.	Present land use %	Land use change
Typical rents $ — to $ — ☐ Increasing ☐ Stable ☐ Declining	One family	Not likely ☐ Likely ☐
Est. neighborhood apt. vacancy — % ☐ Increasing ☐ Stable ☐ Declining	2–4 family	In process to:
Rent controls ☐ Yes ☐ No ☐ Likely — If yes or likely, describe	Multi–family	
	Commercial	
	( )	

Note: Race and the racial composition of the neighborhood are not appraisal factors.

Neighborhood boundaries and characteristics: _____

Factors that affect the marketability of the properties in the neighborhood (proximity to employment and amenities, employment stability, appeal to market, etc.): _____

NEIGHBORHOOD

The following available listings represent the most current, similar, and proximate competitive properties to the subject property in the subject neighborhood. This analysis is intended to evaluate the inventory currently on the market competing with the subject property in the subject neighborhood and recent price and marketing time trends affecting the subject property. (Listings outside the subject neighborhood are not considered applicable). The listing comparables can be the rental or sale comparables if they are currently for sale.

ITEM	SUBJECT	COMPARABLE LISTING NO. 1	COMPARABLE LISTING NO. 2	COMPARABLE LISTING NO. 3
Address				
Proximity to subject				
Listing price	$	☐ Unf. ☐ Furn. $	☐ Unf. ☐ Furn. $	☐ Unf. ☐ Furn. $
Approximate GBA				
Data source				
# Units/Tot. rms./BR/BA				
Approximate year built				
Approx. days on market				

Comparison of listings to subject property: _____

Market conditions that affect 2–4 family properties in the subject neighborhood (including the above neighborhood indicators of growth rate, property values, demand/supply, and marketing time) and the prevalence and impact in the subject market area regarding loan discounts, interest buydowns and concessions, and identification of trends in listing prices, average days on market and any change over past year, etc.: _____

SITE

Dimensions —	Topography	
Site area — Corner lot ☐ No ☐ Yes	Size	
Specific zoning classification and description	Shape	
Zoning compliance ☐ Legal ☐ Legal nonconforming (Grandfathered use) ☐ Illegal ☐ No zoning	Drainage	
Highest & best use as improved: ☐ Present use ☐ Other use (explain)	View	
	Landscaping	

Utilities	Public	Other	Off–site Improvements	Type	Public	Private	
Electricity	☐		Street		☐	☐	Driveway
Gas	☐		Curb/gutter		☐	☐	Apparent easements
Water	☐		Sidewalk		☐	☐	FEMA Special Flood Hazard Area ☐ Yes ☐ No
Sanitary sewer	☐		Street lights		☐	☐	FEMA Zone — Map Date
Storm sewer	☐		Alley		☐	☐	FEMA Map No.

COMMENTS

Comments (apparent adverse easements, encroachments, special assessments, slide areas, illegal or legal nonconforming zoning, use, etc.): _____

The Smart Money Guide to Buying a Home

<table>
<tr><td>General description</td><td colspan="2">Exterior description (Materials/condition)</td><td colspan="2">Foundation</td><td colspan="2">Insulation (R-value if known)</td></tr>
<tr><td>Units/bldgs.   /</td><td colspan="2">Foundation</td><td colspan="2">Slab</td><td>☐ Roof</td><td></td></tr>
<tr><td>Stories</td><td colspan="2">Exterior walls</td><td colspan="2">Crawl space</td><td>☐ Ceiling</td><td></td></tr>
<tr><td>Type (det./att.)</td><td colspan="2">Roof surface</td><td colspan="2">Sump Pump</td><td>☐ Walls</td><td></td></tr>
<tr><td>Design (style)</td><td colspan="2">Gutters & dwnspts.</td><td colspan="2">Dampness</td><td>☐ Floor</td><td></td></tr>
<tr><td>Existing/proposed</td><td colspan="2">Window type</td><td colspan="2">Settlement</td><td>☐ None</td><td></td></tr>
<tr><td>Under construction</td><td colspan="2">Storm sash/Screens</td><td colspan="2">Infestation</td><td>Adequacy</td><td></td></tr>
<tr><td>Year Built</td><td colspan="2">Manufactured housing*   ☐ Yes   ☐ No</td><td colspan="2">Basement   % of 1st floor area</td><td>Energy efficient items:</td><td></td></tr>
<tr><td>Effective age(yrs.)</td><td colspan="2">*(Complies with the HUD Manufactured Housing Construction and Safety Standards.)</td><td colspan="2">Basement finish</td><td></td><td></td></tr>
</table>

DESCRIPTION OF IMPROVEMENTS

Units	Level(s)	Foyer	Living	Dining	Kitchen	Den	Family rm.	Bedrooms	# Baths	Laundry	Other	Sq. ft./unit	Total ☑

Improvements contain: _____ Rooms; _____ Bedroom(s); _____ Bath(s); _____ Square feet of GROSS BUILDING AREA

GROSS BUILDING AREA (GBA) IS DEFINED AS THE TOTAL FINISHED AREA (INCLUDING COMMON AREAS) OF THE IMPROVEMENTS BASED UPON EXTERIOR MEASUREMENTS.

<table>
<tr><td>Surfaces   (Materials/condition)</td><td>Heating</td><td>Kitchen equip. (# / unit – cond.)</td><td>Attic</td><td>Car Storage   No. Cars</td></tr>
<tr><td>Floors</td><td>Type</td><td>Refrigerator</td><td>☐ None</td><td>Garage ☐</td></tr>
<tr><td>Walls</td><td>Fuel</td><td>Range/oven</td><td>☐ Stairs</td><td>Carport ☐</td></tr>
<tr><td>Trim/finish</td><td>Condition</td><td>Disposal</td><td>☐ Drop stair</td><td>Attached ☐</td></tr>
<tr><td>Bath floor</td><td></td><td>Dishwasher</td><td>☐ Scuttle</td><td>Detached ☐</td></tr>
<tr><td>Bath wainscot</td><td>Cooling</td><td>Fan/hood</td><td>☐ Floor</td><td>Adequate ☐</td></tr>
<tr><td>Doors</td><td>Central</td><td>Compactor</td><td>☐ Heated</td><td>Inadequate ☐</td></tr>
<tr><td></td><td>Other</td><td>Washer/dryer</td><td>☐ Finished</td><td>Offstreet ☐</td></tr>
<tr><td></td><td>Condition</td><td>Microwave</td><td>☐ Unfinished</td><td>None ☐</td></tr>
<tr><td>Fireplace(s)   #</td><td></td><td>Intercom</td><td></td><td></td></tr>
</table>

Condition of the improvements, repairs needed, quality of construction, additional feature, modernization, etc.

_____

ADDITIONAL COMMENTS

Depreciation (physical, functional, and external inadequacies, etc.):

_____

Adverse environmental conditions (such as, but not limited to, hazardous wastes, toxic substances, etc.) present in the improvements, on the site, or in the immediate vicinity of the subject property:

_____

VALUATION ANALYSIS

COST APPROACH

ESTIMATED SITE VALUE . . . . = $ _____

ESTIMATED REPRODUCTION COST--NEW OF IMPROVEMENTS:

_____ Sq. Ft. @ $ _____	= $ _____
_____ Sq. Ft. @ $ _____	= $ _____
_____ Sq. Ft. @ $ _____	= $ _____
_____ Sq. Ft. @ $ _____	= $ _____
_____ Sq. Ft. @ $ _____	= $ _____
	= $ _____
	= $ _____
	= $ _____
	= $ _____

Special Energy Efficient Items _____ = $ _____

Porches, Patios, etc. _____ = $ _____

Total Estimated Cost New . . . . = $ _____

	Physical	Functional	External
Less Depreciation			

Depreciation _____ = $ _____

Depreciated Value of Improvements . . . . = $ _____

"As is" Value of Site Improvements . . . . = $ _____

INDICATED VALUE BY COST APPROACH . . . . = $ _____

Comments on Cost Approach (such as, source of cost estimate, site value, square foot calculation and, for HUD and VA, the estimated remaining economic life of the property): _____

128

Appendix F

At least three rental comparables should be reported and analyzed in this section. The rental comparables should represent the most current rental information on properties as similar and proximate to the subject property as possible. (This comparison is based on current rental data, therefore, the rental comparables typically are not the same comparables used in the sales comparison analysis.) The appraisal report should assure the reader that the units and properties selected as comparables are comparable to the subject property (both the units and the overall property) and accurately represent the rental market for the subject property (unless otherwise stated within the report).

ITEM	SUBJECT	COMPARABLE RENTAL NO. 1	COMPARABLE RENTAL NO. 2	COMPARABLE RENTAL NO. 3
Address				
Proximity to subject				
Lease dates (if available)				
Rent survey date				
Data source				
Rent concessions				

Description of property--units, design, appeal, age, vacancies, and conditions	No. Units No. Vac. Yr. Blt.:	No. Units No. Vac. Yr. Blt.:	No. Units No. Vac. Yr. Blt.:	No. Units No. Vac. Yr. Blt.:

	Rm. Count (Tot Br Ba)	Size Sq. Ft.	Rm. Count (Tot Br Ba)	Size Sq. Ft.	Total Monthly Rent	Rm. Count (Tot Br Ba)	Size Sq. Ft.	Total Monthly Rent	Rm. Count (Tot Br Ba)	Size Sq. Ft.	Total Monthly Rent
Individual Unit breakdown											

Utilities, furniture, and amenities included in rent

Functional utility, basement, heating/cooling, project amenities, etc.

Analysis of rental data and support for estimated market rents for the individual subject units (including the adjustments used, the adequacy of comparables, rental concessions, etc.)

Subject's rent schedule The rent schedule reconciles the applicable indicated monthly market rents to the appropriate subject unit, and provides the estimated rents for the subject property. The appraiser must review the rent characteristics of the comparable sales to determine whether estimated rents should reflect actual or market rents. For example, if actual rents were available on the sales comparables and used to derive the gross rent multiplier (GRM), actual rents for the subject should be used. If market rents were used to construct the comparables' rents and derive the GRM, market rents should be used. The total gross estimated rent must represent rent characteristics consistent with the sales comparable data used to derive the GRM. The total gross estimated rent is not adjusted for vacancy.

Unit	LEASES Lease Date Begin	End	No. Units Vacant	ACTUAL RENTS Per Unit Unfurnished	Furnished	Total Rents	ESTIMATED RENTS Per Unit Unfurnished	Furnished	Total Rents
				$	$	$	$	$	$
						$			$

Other monthly income (itemize) _____ $ _____

Vacancy: Actual last year _____ % Previous year _____ % Estimated: _____ % $ _____ Annually   **Total gross estimated rent $** _____

Utilities included in estimated rents: ☐ Electric ☐ Water ☐ Sewer ☐ Gas ☐ Oil ☐ Trash collection _____

Comments on the rent schedule, actual rents, estimated rents (especially regarding differences between actual and estimated rents), utilities, etc.: _____

129

SALES COMPARISON ANALYSIS

The undersigned has recited three recent sales of properties most similar and proximate to the subject property and has described and analyzed these in this analysis. If there is a significant variation between the subject and comparable properties, the analysis includes a dollar adjustment reflecting the market reaction to those items or an explanation supported by the market data. If a significant item in the comparable property is superior to, or more favorable than, the subject property, a minus (-) adjustment is made, thus reducing the adjusted sales price of the comparable property; if a significant item in the comparable property is inferior to, or less favorable than, the subject property, a plus (+) adjustment is made, thus increasing the adjusted sales price of the comparable property. **[(1) Sales Price / Gross Monthly Rent]**

ITEM	SUBJECT	COMPARABLE SALE NO. 1	COMPARABLE SALE NO. 2	COMPARABLE SALE NO. 3
Address				
Proximity to subject				
Sales price	$	☐ Unf. ☐ Furn. $	☐ Unf. ☐ Furn. $	☐ Unf. ☐ Furn. $
Sales price per GBA	$	$	$	$
Gross monthly rent	$	$	$	$
Gross mo. rent mult. (1)				
Sales price per unit	$	$	$	$
Sales price per room	$	$	$	$
Data and/or Verification Sources				

ADJUSTMENTS	DESCRIPTION	DESCRIPTION	+ (-) $ Adjustment	DESCRIPTION	+ (-) $ Adjustment	DESCRIPTION	+ (-) $ Adjustment
Sales or financing concessions							
Date of sale/time							
Location							
Leasehold/Fee Simple							
Site							
View							
Design and appeal							
Quality of construction							
Age							
Condition							
Gross Building Area	Sq. ft.	Sq. Ft.		Sq. Ft.		Sq. Ft.	
Unit breakdown	No. of units / Rm. Count (Tot, Br, Ba) / No. Vac.	No. of units / Rm. Count (Tot, Br, Ba) / No. Vac.		No. of units / Rm. Count (Tot, Br, Ba) / No. Vac.		No. of units / Rm. Count (Tot, Br, Ba) / No. Vac.	
Basement description							
Functional utility							
Heating/cooling							
Parking on/off site							
Project amenities and fee (if applicable)							
Net Adj. (total)		☐ + ☐ - $		☐ + ☐ - $		☐ + ☐ - $	
Adjusted sales price of comparable			$		$		$

Comments on sales comparison (including reconciliation of all indicators of value as to consistency and relative strength and evaluation of the typical investor's/purchaser's motivation in that market):

ITEM	SUBJECT	COMPARABLE NO. 1	COMPARABLE NO. 2	COMPARABLE NO. 3
Date, Price and Data Source for prior sales within year of appraisal				

Analysis of any current agreement of sale, option, or listing of the subject property and analysis of any prior sales of subject and comparables within one year of the date of appraisal:

INC

Total gross monthly estimated rent $ ______ x gross rent multiplier (GRM) ______ = $ ______ INDICATED VALUE BY INCOME APPROACH

Comments on income approach (including expense ratios, if available, and reconciliation of the GRM)

RECONCILIATION

INDICATED VALUE BY SALES COMPARISON APPROACH . . . . $ ______

INDICATED VALUE BY INCOME APPROACH . . . . $ ______

INDICATED VALUE BY COST APPROACH . . . . $ ______

This appraisal is made ☐ "as is" ☐ subject to the repairs, alterations, inspections, or conditions listed below ☐ subject to completion per plans and specifications.

Comments and conditions of appraisal:

Final reconciliation:

The purpose of this appraisal is to estimate the market value of the real property that is the subject of this report, based on the above conditions and the certification, contingent and limiting conditions, and market value definition that are stated in the attached Freddie Mac Form 439/Fannie Mae Form 1004B (Revised ______).

I (WE) ESTIMATE THE MARKET VALUE, AS DEFINED, OF THE REAL PROPERTY THAT IS THE SUBJECT OF THIS REPORT, AS OF ______ (WHICH IS THE DATE OF INSPECTION AND THE EFFECTIVE DATE OF THIS REPORT) TO BE $ ______

APPRAISER:		**SUPERVISORY APPRAISER (ONLY IF REQUIRED):**	
Signature		Signature	☐ Did ☐ Did Not
Name		Name	Inspect Property
Date Report Signed		Date Report Signed	
State Certification #	State	State Certification #	State
Or State License #	State	Or State License #	State

Appendix G
Statement of Limiting Conditions and Appraiser's Certification

DEFINITION OF MARKET VALUE: The most probable price which a property should bring in a competitive and open market under all conditions requisite to a fair sale, the buyer and seller, each acting prudently, knowledgeably and assuming the price is not affected by undue stimulus. Implicit in this definition is the consummation of a sale as of a specified date and the passing of title from seller to buyer under conditions whereby: (1) buyer and seller are typically motivated; (2) both parties are well informed or well advised, and each acting in what he considers his own best interest; (3) a reasonable time is allowed for exposure in the open market; (4) payment is made in terms of cash in U.S. dollars or in terms of financial arrangements comparable thereto; and (5) the price represents the normal consideration for the property sold unaffected by special or creative financing or sales concessions* granted by anyone associated with the sale.

*Adjustments to the comparables must be made for special or creative financing or sales concessions. No adjustments are necessary for those costs which are normally paid by sellers as a result of tradition or law in a market area; these costs are readily identifiable since the seller pays these costs in virtually all sales transactions. Special or creative financing adjustments can be made to the comparable property by comparisons to financing terms offered by a third party institutional lender that is not already involved in the property or transaction. Any adjustment should not be calculated on a mechanical dollar for dollar cost of the financing or concession but the dollar amount of any adjustment should approximate the market's reaction to the financing or concessions based on the appraiser's judgment.

STATEMENT OF LIMITING CONDITIONS AND APPRAISER'S CERTIFICATION

CONTINGENT AND LIMITING CONDITIONS: The appraiser's certification that appears in the appraisal report is subject to the following conditions:

1. The appraiser will not be responsible for matters of a legal nature that affect either the property being appraised or the title to it. The appraiser assumes that the title is good and marketable and, therefore, will not render any opinions about the title. The property is appraised on the basis of it being under responsible ownership.

2. The appraiser has provided a sketch in the appraisal report to show approximate dimensions of the improvements and the sketch is included only to assist the reader of the report in visualizing the property and understanding the appraiser's determination of its size.

3. The appraiser has examined the available flood maps that are provided by the Federal Emergency Management Agency (or other data sources) and has noted in the appraisal report whether the subject site is located in an identified Special Flood Hazard Area. Because the appraiser is not a surveyor, he or she makes no guarantees, express or implied, regarding this determination.

4. The appraiser will not give testimony or appear in court because he or she made an appraisal of the property in question, unless specific arrangements to do so have been made beforehand.

5. The appraiser has estimated the value of the land in the cost approach at its highest and best use and the improvements at their contributory value. These separate valuations of the land and improvements must not be used in conjunction with any other appraisal and are invalid if they are so used.

6. The appraiser has noted in the appraisal report any adverse conditions (such as, needed repairs, depreciation, the presence of hazardous wastes, toxic substances, etc.) observed during the inspection of the subject property or that he or she became aware of during the normal research involved in performing the appraisal. Unless otherwise stated in the appraisal report, the appraiser has no knowledge of any hidden or unapparent conditions of the property or adverse environmental conditions (including the presence of hazardous wastes, toxic substances, etc.) that would make the property more or less valuable, and has assumed that there are no such conditions and makes no guarantees or warranties, express or implied, regarding the condition of the property. The appraiser will not be responsible for any such conditions that do exist or for any engineering or testing that might be required to discover whether such conditions exist. Because the appraiser is not an expert in the field of environmental hazards, the appraisal report must not be considered as an environmental assessment of the property.

7. The appraiser obtained the information, estimates, and opinions that were expressed in the appraisal report from sources that he or she considers to be reliable and believes them to be true and correct. The appraiser does not assume responsibility for the accuracy of such items that were furnished by other parties.

8. The appraiser will not disclose the contents of the appraisal report except as provided for in the Uniform Standards of Professional Appraisal Practice.

9. The appraiser has based his or her appraisal report and valuation conclusion for an appraisal that is subject to satisfactory completion, repairs, or alterations on the assumption that completion of the improvements will be performed in a workmanlike manner.

10. The appraiser must provide his or her prior written consent before the lender/client specified in the appraisal report can distribute the appraisal report (including conclusions about the property value, the appraiser's identity and professional designations, and references to any professional appraisal organizations or the firm with which the appraiser is associated) to anyone other than the borrower; the mortgagee or its successors and assigns; the mortgage insurer; consultants; professional appraisal organizations; any state or federally approved financial institution; or any department, agency, or instrumentality of the United States or any state or the District of Columbia; except that the lender/client may distribute the property description section of the report only to data collection or reporting service(s) without having to obtain the appraiser's prior written consent. The appraiser's written consent and approval must also be obtained before the appraisal can be conveyed by anyone to the public through advertising, public relations, news, sales, or other media.

The Smart Money Guide to Buying a Home

APPRAISER'S CERTIFICATION: The Appraiser certifies and agrees that:

1. I have researched the subject market area and have selected a minimum of three recent sales of properties most similar and proximate to the subject property for consideration in the sales comparison analysis and have made a dollar adjustment when appropriate to reflect the market reaction to those items of significant variation. If a significant item in a comparable property is superior to, or more favorable than, the subject property, I have made a negative adjustment to reduce the adjusted sales price of the comparable and, if a significant item in a comparable property is inferior to, or less favorable than the subject property, I have made a positive adjustment to increase the adjusted sales price of the comparable.

2. I have taken into consideration the factors that have an impact on value in my development of the estimate of market value in the appraisal report. I have not knowingly withheld any significant information from the appraisal report and I believe, to the best of my knowledge, that all statements and information in the appraisal report are true and correct.

3. I stated in the appraisal report only my own personal, unbiased, and professional analysis, opinions, and conclusions, which are subject only to the contingent and limiting conditions specified in this form.

4. I have no present or prospective interest in the property that is the subject to this report, and I have no present or prospective personal interest or bias with respect to the participants in the transaction. I did not base, either partially or completely, my analysis and/or the estimate of market value in the appraisal report on the race, color, religion, sex, handicap, familial status, or national origin of either the prospective owners or occupants of the subject property or of the present owners or occupants of the properties in the vicinity of the subject property.

5. I have no present or contemplated future interest in the subject property, and neither my current or future employment nor my compensation for performing this appraisal is contingent on the appraised value of the property.

6. I was not required to report a predetermined value or direction in value that favors the cause of the client or any related party, the amount of the value estimate, the attainment of a specific result, or the occurrence of a subsequent event in order to receive my compensation and/or employment for performing the appraisal. I did not base the appraisal report on a requested minimum valuation, a specific valuation, or the need to approve a specific mortgage loan.

7. I performed this appraisal in conformity with the Uniform Standards of Professional Appraisal Practice that were adopted and promulgated by the Appraisal Standards Board of The Appraisal Foundation and that were in place as of the effective date of this appraisal, with the exception of the departure provision of those Standards, which does not apply. I acknowledge that an estimate of a reasonable time for exposure in the open market is a condition in the definition of market value and the estimate I developed is consistent with the marketing time noted in the neighborhood section of this report, unless I have otherwise stated in the reconciliation section.

8. I have personally inspected the interior and exterior areas of the subject property and the exterior of all properties listed as comparables in the appraisal report. I further certify that I have noted any apparent or known adverse conditions in the subject improvements, on the subject site, or on any site within the immediate vicinity of the subject property of which I am aware and have made adjustments for these adverse conditions in my analysis of the property value to the extent that I had market evidence to support them. I have also commented about the effect of the adverse conditions on the marketability of the subject property.

9. I personally prepared all conclusions and opinions about the real estate that were set forth in the appraisal report. If I relied on significant professional assistance from any individual or individuals in the performance of the appraisal or the preparation of the appraisal report, I have named such individual(s) and disclosed the specific tasks performed by them in the reconciliation section of this appraisal report. I certify that any individual so named is qualified to perform the tasks. I have not authorized anyone to make a change to any item in the report; therefore, if an unauthorized change is made to the appraisal report, I will take no responsibility for it.

SUPERVISORY APPRAISER'S CERTIFICATION: If a supervisory appraiser signed the appraisal report, he or she certifies and agrees that: I directly supervise the appraiser who prepared the appraisal report, have reviewed the appraisal report, agree with the statements and conclusions of the appraiser, agree to be bound by the appraiser's certifications number 4 through 7 above, and am taking full responsibility for the appraisal and the appraisal report.

ADDRESS OF PROPERTY APPRAISED: _____

APPRAISER:

Signature: _____
Name: _____
Date Signed: _____
State Certification #: _____
or State License #: _____
State: _____
Expiration Date of Certification or License: _____

SUPERVISORY APPRAISER (only if required):

Signature: _____
Name: _____
Date Signed: _____
State Certification #: _____
or State License #: _____
State: _____
Expiration Date of Certification or License: _____

☐ Did ☐ Did Not Inspect Property

Appendix H
Contract for Sale and Purchase

Residential Sale and Purchase Contract
FLORIDA ASSOCIATION OF REALTORS®

PRICE AND FINANCING

1* **1. SALE AND PURCHASE:** _____ ("Seller")
2* and _____ ("Buyer")
3 agree to sell and buy on the terms and conditions specified below the property described as:
4* Address: _____
5* _____ County: _____
6* Legal Description: _____
7* _____ Tax ID No: _____
8 together with all improvements and attached items, including fixtures, built-in furnishings, built-in appliances, ceiling fans,
9 light fixtures, attached wall-to-wall carpeting, rods, draperies and other window coverings. The only other items included
10* in the purchase are: _____
11* _____
12* _____
13* The following attached items are excluded from the purchase: _____
14* _____
15 The real and personal property described above as included in the purchase is referred to as the "Property." Personal property listed
16 in this Contract is included in the purchase price, has no contributory value and is being left for **Seller's** convenience.

17 **PRICE AND FINANCING**
18* **2. PURCHASE PRICE:** $ _____ payable by **Buyer** in U.S. currency as follows:
19* **(a)** $ _____ Deposit received (checks are subject to clearance) _____ by
20* _____ for ("Escrow Agent") _____
21 _____ Signature _____ Name of Company
22* **(b)** $ _____ Additional deposit to be made by _____
23* **(c)** _____ Total Financing (see Paragraph **3** below) (express as a dollar amount or percentage)
24* **(d)** $ _____ Other: _____
25* **(e)** $ _____ Balance to close (not including **Buyer's** closing costs, prepaid items and prorations). All funds
26 paid at closing must be paid by locally drawn cashier's check or official bank check or wired
27 funds.
28 **3. FINANCING:** (Check as applicable) ☐ **(a) Buyer** will pay cash for the Property with no financing contingency. ☐ **(b)** This
29* Contract is contingent on **Buyer** qualifying and obtaining **(1)** and /or **(2)** below (the "Financing") by _____
30* (if left blank then Closing Date or within 30 days from Effective Date, whichever occurs first) ("Financing Period"):
31* ☐ **(1)** A commitment for new ☐ conventional ☐ FHA ☐ VA financing for $ _____ or _____ % of the purchase price (plus
32 any applicable PMI, MIP, VA funding fee) at the prevailing interest rate and loan costs (if FHA or VA, see attached addendum).
33* ☐ **(2)** Approval for **Seller** financing or assumption of mortgage (see attached addendum).
34* **Buyer** will apply for Financing within _____ days from Effective Date (5 days if left blank) and will timely provide any and all credit,
35 employment, financial and other information required by the lender. Either party may cancel this Contract if **(i) Buyer**, after using
36 diligence and good faith, cannot obtain the Financing, (including meeting the terms of the commitment), or **(ii)** the Financing
37 is denied because the Property appraises below the purchase price and either **Buyer** elects not to proceed or the parties are
38 unable to renegotiate the purchase price. Upon cancellation, **Buyer** will return all **Seller**-provided title evidence, surveys and
39 association documents and **Buyer's** deposit(s) will be returned after Escrow Agent receives proper authorization from all
40 interested parties.

41 **CLOSING**
42* **4. CLOSING DATE; OCCUPANCY**: This Contract will be closed and the deed and possession delivered on _____
43 ("Closing Date"), unless extended by other provisions of this Contract. The Property will be swept clean and **Seller's** personal items
44 removed on or before Closing Date. If on Closing Date insurance underwriting is suspended, **Buyer** may postpone closing up to 5 days.
45 **5. CLOSING PROCEDURE; COSTS**: Closing will take place in the county where the Property is located. If title insurance
46 insures **Buyer** for title defects arising between the title binder effective date and recording of **Buyer's** deed, closing agent will
47 disburse at closing the net sale proceeds to **Seller** and brokerage fees to Broker as per Paragraph **19**. In addition to other
48 expenses provided in this Contract, **Seller** and **Buyer** will pay the costs indicated below.
49 **(a) Seller Costs: Seller** will pay taxes and surtaxes on the deed and recording fees for documents needed to cure title; certified,
50 confirmed and ratified special assessment liens; and, if an improvement is substantially completed as of Effective Date, an
51* amount equal to the last estimate of the assessment; up to _____ % (1.5% if left blank) of the purchase price for repairs to
52* warranted items **("Repair Limit")**; and up to _____ % (1.5% if left blank) of the purchase price for wood-destroying organism
53* treatment and repairs **("Termite Repair Limit")**; Other: _____
54 **(b) Buyer Costs: Buyer** will pay taxes and recording fees on notes and mortgages; recording fees on the deed and
55 financing statements; loan expenses; pending special assessment liens; lender's title policy; inspections; survey; flood
56* insurance; Other: _____
57 **(c) Title Evidence and Insurance: Check (1) or (2):**
58* ☐ **(1) Seller** will provide a Paragraph 10(a)(1) owner's title insurance commitment as title evidence. ☐ **Seller** ☐ **Buyer** will
59* select the title agent. ☐ **Seller** ☐ **Buyer** will pay for the owner's title policy, search, examination and related charges.
60 Each party will pay its own closing costs.
61* ☐ **(2) Seller** will provide title evidence as specified in Paragraph 10(a)(2). ☐ **Seller** ☐ **Buyer** will pay for the owner's title
62 policy and select the title agent. **Seller** will pay fees for title searches prior to closing, including tax search and lien
63 search fees, and **Buyer** will pay fees for title searches after closing (if any), title examination fees and closing fees.
64 **(d) Prorations:** The following items will be made current (if applicable) and prorated as of the day before Closing Date: real
65 estate taxes, interest, bonds, assessments, association fees, insurance, rents and other current expenses and revenues of
66 the Property. If taxes and assessments for the current year cannot be determined, the previous year's rates will be used with
67 adjustment for exemptions and improvements. **Buyer** is responsible for property tax increases due to change in ownership.
68 **(e) Tax Withholding: Buyer** and **Seller** will comply with the Foreign Investment in Real Property Tax Act, which may require
69 **Seller** to provide additional cash at closing if **Seller** is a "foreign person" as defined by federal law.
70* **(f) Home Warranty:** ☐ **Buyer** ☐ **Seller** ☐ **N/A** will pay for a home warranty plan issued by _____ at a
71* cost not to exceed $ _____ . A home warranty plan provides for repair or replacement of many of a home's mechanical
72 systems and major built-in appliances in the event of breakdown due to normal wear and tear during the agreement period.

73 **PROPERTY CONDITION**
74* **6. INSPECTION PERIODS: Buyer** will complete the inspections referenced in Paragraphs **7** and **8(a)(2)** by _____
75* (within 10 days from Effective Date if left blank) ("Inspection Period"), the wood-destroying organism inspection by
76* _____ (prior to closing if left blank), and the walk-through inspection on the day before Closing Date
77 or any other time agreeable to the parties.

78* **Buyer** (_____)(_____) and **Seller** (_____)(_____) acknowledge receipt of a copy of this page, which is Page 1 of 4 Pages.

FAR-5 Rev. 10/98 ©1998 Florida Association of Realtors® All Rights Reserved
This form is licensed for use with **Formulator®** Forms Software by ISG McAllister Publishing, Inc. 800-336-1027

.79   **7. REAL PROPERTY DISCLOSURE: Seller** represents that **Seller** does not know of any facts that materially affect the value of
80   the Property, including violations of governmental laws, rules and regulations, other than those that **Buyer** can readily observe
81   or that are known by or have been disclosed to **Buyer.**
82   **(a) Energy Efficiency: Buyer** acknowledges receipt of the Florida Building Energy-Efficiency Rating System brochure. If
83   this is a new home, the builder's FL-EPL card is attached as an addendum.
84   **(b) Radon Gas:** Radon is a naturally occurring radioactive gas that, when it has accumulated in a building in sufficient
86   quantities, may present health risks to persons who are exposed to it over time. Levels of radon that exceed federal and
87   state guidelines have been found in buildings in Florida. Additional information regarding radon and radon testing may be
88   obtained from your county public health unit. **Buyer** may, within the Inspection Period, have an appropriately licensed person
89   test the Property for radon. If the radon level exceeds acceptable EPA standards, **Seller** may choose to reduce the radon
90   level to an acceptable EPA level, failing which either party may cancel this Contract.
91   **(c) Flood Zone: Buyer** is advised to verify by survey, with the lender and with appropriate government agencies which flood
92   zone the Property is in, whether flood insurance is required and what restrictions apply to improving the Property and rebuilding
93   in the event of casualty. If the Property is in a Special Flood Hazard Area or Coastal High Hazard Area and the buildings are built
94   below the minimum flood elevation, **Buyer** may cancel this Contract by delivering written notice to notice to **Seller** within 20 days
96   from Effective Date, failing which **Buyer** accepts the existing elevation of the buildings and zone designation of the Property.
97   **(d) Homeowner's Association:** If membership in a homeowner's association is mandatory, an association disclosure
98   summary is attached and incorporated into this contract. **BUYER** SHOULD NOT SIGN THIS CONTRACT UNTIL **BUYER**
99   HAS RECEIVED AND READ THE DISCLOSURE SUMMARY.
100 **8. MAINTENANCE, INSPECTIONS AND REPAIR: Seller** will keep the Property in the same condition from Effective Date until
101 closing, except for normal wear and tear ("maintenance requirement") and repairs required by this Contract. **Seller** will provide
102 access and utilities for **Buyer's** inspections. **Buyer** will repair all damages to the Property resulting from the inspections and
103 return the Property to its preinspection condition. If **Seller** is unable to complete required repairs or treatment prior to
104 closing, **Seller** will give **Buyer** a credit at closing for the cost of the repairs **Seller** was obligated to make. **Seller** will assign all
105 assignable repair and treatment contracts to **Buyer** at closing.
106   **(a) Warranty, Inspections and Repair:**
107   **(1) Warranty: Seller** warrants that non-leased major appliances and heating, cooling, mechanical, electrical, security,
108   sprinkler, septic and plumbing systems, seawall, dock and pool equipment, if any, are and will be maintained in working
109   condition until closing; that the structures (including roofs) and pool, if any, are structurally sound and watertight; and
110   that the Property has proper permits. **Seller** does not warrant and is not required to repair cosmetic conditions, unless
111   the cosmetic condition resulted from a defect in a warranted item. **Seller** is not obligated to bring any item into
112   compliance with existing building code regulations unless necessary to repair a warranted item. "Working condition"
113   means operating in the manner in which the item was designed to operate and "cosmetic conditions" means aesthetic
114   imperfections that do not affect the working condition of the item, including pitted marcite; missing or torn screens;
115   fogged windows; tears, worn spots and discoloration of floor coverings / wallpapers / window treatments; nail holes,
116   scratches, dents, scrapes, chips and caulking in bathroom ceiling / walls / flooring / tile / fixtures / mirrors; and minor cracks in
117   floor tiles / windows / driveways / sidewalks / pool decks / garage and patio floors.
118   **(2) Professional Inspection: Buyer** may have warranted items inspected by a person who specializes in and holds an
119   occupational license (if required by law) to conduct home inspections or who holds a Florida license to repair and maintain
120   the items inspected ("professional inspector"). **Buyer** must, within 5 days from the end of the Inspection Period, deliver
121   written notice of any items that are not in the condition warranted and a copy of the inspector's written report, if any, to
122   **Seller.** If **Buyer** fails to deliver timely written notice, **Buyer** waives **Seller's** warranty and accepts the items listed in
123   subparagraph (a) in their "as is" conditions, except that **Seller** must meet the maintenance requirement.
124   **(3) Repair: Seller** is obligated only to make repairs necessary to bring warranted items into the condition warranted, up
125   to the Repair Limit. **Seller** may, within 5 days from receipt of **Buyer's** notice of items that are not in the condition
126   warranted, have a second inspection made by a professional inspector and will report repair estimates to **Buyer.** If the
127   first and second inspection reports differ and the parties cannot resolve the differences, **Buyer** and **Seller** together will
128   choose, and equally split the cost of, a third inspector, whose written report will be binding on the parties. If the cost to
129   repair warranted items equals or is less than the Repair Limit, **Seller** will have the repairs made in a workmanlike manner
130   by an appropriately licensed person. If the cost to repair warranted items exceeds the Repair Limit, either party may
131   cancel this Contract unless either party pays the excess or **Buyer** designates which repairs to make at a total cost to
132   **Seller** not exceeding the Repair Limit and accepts the balance of the Property in its "as is" condition.
133   **(b) Wood-Destroying Organisms:** "Wood-destroying organism" means arthropod or plant life, including termites, powder-post
134   beetles, oldhouse borers and wood-decaying fungi, that damages or infests seasoned wood in a structure, excluding fences.
135   **Buyer** may, at **Buyer's** expense and prior to closing, have the Property inspected by a Florida-licensed pest control business to
136   determine the existence of past or present wood-destroying organism infestation and damage caused by infestation. If the
137   inspector finds evidence of infestation or damage, **Buyer** will deliver a copy of the inspector's written report to **Seller** within 5
138   days from the date of the inspection. **Seller** is not obligated to treat the Property if all of the following apply (i) there is no
139   visible live infestation, (ii) the Property has previously been treated, and (iii) **Seller** transfers a current full treatment
140   warranty to **Buyer** at closing. Otherwise, **Seller** will have 5 days from receipt of the inspector's report to have reported
141   damage estimated by a licensed building or general contractor and corrective treatment estimated by a licensed pest
142   control business. **Seller** will have treatments and repairs made by an appropriately licensed person at **Seller's** expense up
143   to the Termite Repair Limit. If the cost to treat and repair the Property exceeds the Termite Repair Limit, either party may
144   pay the excess, failing which either party may cancel this Contract. If **Buyer** fails to timely deliver the inspector's written
145   report, **Buyer** accepts the Property "as is" with regard to wood-destroying organism infestation and damage, subject to the
146   maintenance requirement.
147   **(c) Walk-through Inspection: Buyer** may walk through the Property solely to verify that **Seller** has made repairs required
148   by this Contract and has met contractual obligations. No other issues may be raised as a result of the walk-through
149   inspection. If **Buyer** fails to conduct this inspection, **Seller's** repair and maintenance obligations will be deemed fulfilled.
150 **9. RISK OF LOSS:** If any portion of the Property is damaged by fire or other casualty before closing and can be restored
151 within 45 days from the Closing Date to substantially the same condition as it was on Effective Date, **Seller** will, at **Seller's**
152 expense, restore the Property and the Closing Date will be extended accordingly. If the restoration cannot be completed in
153 time, **Buyer** may accept the Property "as is" with **Seller** assigning the insurance proceeds for the Property to **Buyer** at closing,
154 failing which either party may cancel this Contract.
155   **TITLE**
156 **10. TITLE: Seller** will convey marketable title to the Property by statutory warranty deed or trustee, personal representative or
157 guardian deed as appropriate to **Seller's** status.
158   **(a) Title Evidence:** Title evidence will show legal access to the Property and marketable title of record in **Seller** in accordance with
159   current title standards adopted by the Florida Bar, subject only to the following title exceptions, none of which prevent residential
160   use of the Property: covenants, easements and restrictions of record; matters of plat; existing zoning and government
161   regulations; oil, gas and mineral rights of record if there is no right of entry; current taxes; mortgages that **Buyer** will assume; and
162   encumbrances that **Seller** will discharge at or before closing. **Seller** will, prior to closing, deliver to **Buyer Seller's** choice of one of
163   the following types of title evidence, which must be generally accepted in the county where the Property is located (specify in
164   Paragraph 5(c) the selected type). **Seller** will use option (1) in Palm Beach County and option (2) in Dade County.
165   **(1) A title insurance commitment** issued by a Florida-licenced title insurer in the amount of the purchase price and
166   subject only to title exceptions set forth in this Contract.

167* **Buyer** (_____)(_____) and **Seller** (_____)(_____) acknowledge receipt of a copy of this page, which is Page 2 of 4 Pages.

168   **(2) An existing abstract of title** from a reputable and existing abstract firm (if firm is not existing, then abstract must be
169   certified as correct by an existing firm) purporting to be an accurate synopsis of the instruments affecting title to the
170   Property recorded in the public records of the county where the Property is located and certified to Effective Date.
171   However if such an abstract is not available to **Seller**, then a **prior owner's title policy** acceptable to the proposed insurer
172   as a base for reissuance of coverage. **Seller** will pay for copies of all policy exceptions and an update in a format
173   acceptable to **Buyer's** closing agent from the policy effective date and certified to **Buyer** or **Buyer's** closing agent,
174   together with copies of all documents recited in the prior policy and in the update. If a prior policy is not available to
175   **Seller** then (1) above will be the title evidence. Title evidence will be delivered no later than 10 days before Closing Date.
176   **(b) Title Examination:** Buyer will examine the title evidence and deliver written notice to **Seller**, within 5 days from receipt of
177   title evidence but no later than closing, of any defects that make the title unmarketable. **Seller** will have 30 days from
178   receipt of **Buyer's** notice of defects ("Curative Period") to cure the defects at **Seller's** expense. If **Seller** cures the defects
179   within the Curative Period, **Seller** will deliver written notice to **Buyer** and the parties will close the transaction on Closing
180   Date or within 10 days from **Buyer's** receipt of **Seller's** notice if Closing Date has passed. If **Seller** is unable to cure the
181   defects within the Curative Period, **Seller** will deliver written notice to **Buyer** and **Buyer** will, within 10 days from receipt of
182   **Seller's** notice, either cancel this Contract or accept title with existing defects and close the transaction.
183   **(c) Survey:** Buyer may, prior to Closing Date and at **Buyer's** expense, have the Property surveyed and deliver written notice to
184   **Seller**, within 5 days from receipt of survey but no later than closing, of any encroachments on the Property, encroachments by the
185   Property's improvements on other lands or deed restriction or zoning violations. Any such encroachment or violation will be treated
186   in the same manner as a title defect and **Buyer's** and **Seller's** obligations will be determined in accordance with subparagraph (b)
187   above. If any part of the Property lies seaward of the coastal construction control line, **Seller** will provide **Buyer** with an affidavit or
188   survey as required by law delineating the line's location on the property, unless **Buyer** waives this requirement in writing.

189   **MISCELLANEOUS**
190   **11. EFFECTIVE DATE; TIME:** The "Effective Date" of this Contract is the date on which the last of the parties initials or signs the
191   latest offer. **Time is of the essence for all provisions of this Contract.** All time periods will be computed in business days (a
192   "business day" is every calendar day except Saturday, Sunday and national legal holidays). If any deadline falls on a
193   Saturday, Sunday or national legal holiday, performance will be due the next business day. All time periods will
194   end at 5:00 p.m. local time (meaning in the county where the Property is located) of the appropriate day.

195   **12. NOTICES:** All notices will be made to the parties and Broker by mail, personal delivery or electronic media. **Buyer's failure
196   to deliver timely written notice to Seller, when such notice is required by this Contract, regarding any contingencies will render
197   that contingency null and void and the Contract will be construed as if the contingency did not exist.**

198   **13. COMPLETE AGREEMENT:** This Contract is the entire agreement between **Buyer** and **Seller**. **Except for brokerage
199   agreements, no prior or present agreements will bind Buyer, Seller or Broker unless incorporated into this Contract.**
200   Modifications of this Contract will not be binding unless in writing, signed and delivered by the party to be bound. Signatures,
201   initials, documents referenced in this Contract, counterparts and written modifications communicated electronically or on paper
202   will be acceptable for all purposes, including delivery, and will be binding. Handwritten or typewritten terms inserted in or
203   attached to this Contract prevail over preprinted terms. If any provision of this Contract is or becomes invalid or unenforceable
204   all remaining provisions will continue to be fully effective. This Contract will not be recorded in any public records.

205   **14. ASSIGNABILITY; PERSONS BOUND:** Buyer may **not** assign this Contract without **Seller's** written consent. The terms
206   **Buyer," "Seller,"** and "Broker" may be singular or plural. This Contract is binding on the heirs, administrators, executors,
207   personal representatives and assigns (if permitted) of **Buyer, Seller** and Broker.

208   **DEFAULT AND DISPUTE RESOLUTION**
209   **15. DEFAULT: (a) Seller Default:** If for any reason other than failure of **Seller** to make **Seller's** title marketable after diligent effort,
210   **Seller** fails, refuses or neglects to perform this Contract, **Buyer** may choose to receive a return of **Buyer's** deposit without
211   waiving the right to seek damages or to seek specific performance as per Paragraph 16. **Seller** will also be liable to Broker for
212   the full amount of the brokerage fee. **(b) Buyer Default:** If **Buyer** fails to perform this Contract within the time specified, including
213   timely payment of all deposits, **Seller** may choose to retain and collect all deposits paid and agreed to be paid as liquidated
214   damages or to seek specific performance as per Paragraph 16; and Broker will, upon demand, receive 50% of all deposits
215   paid and agreed to be paid (to be split equally among cooperating brokers) up to the full amount of the brokerage fee.

216   **16. DISPUTE RESOLUTION:** This Contract will be construed under Florida law. All controversies, claims and other matters in
217   question arising out of or relating to this transaction or this Contract or its breach will be settled as follows:
218   **(a) Disputes concerning entitlement to deposits made and agreed to be made:** Buyer and Seller will have 30 days from the
219   date conflicting demands are made to attempt to resolve the dispute through **mediation**. If that fails, Escrow Agent will
220   submit the dispute, if so required by Florida law, to Escrow Agent's choice of arbitration, a Florida court or the Florida Real
221   Estate Commission. **Buyer** and **Seller** will be bound by any resulting settlement or order.
222   **(b) All other disputes:** Buyer and Seller will have 30 days from the date a dispute arises between them to attempt to
223   resolve the matter through mediation, failing which the parties will resolve the dispute through neutral binding **arbitration**
224   in the county where the Property is based. The arbitrator may not alter the Contract terms or award any remedy not
225   provided for in this Contract. The award will be based on the greater weight of the evidence and will state findings of fact
226   and the contractual authority on which it is based. If the parties agree to use discovery, it will be in accordance with the
227   Florida Rules of Civil Procedure and the arbitrator will resolve all discovery-related disputes. Any disputes with a real
228   estate licensee named in Paragraph 19 will be submitted to arbitration only if the licensee's broker consents in writing to
229   become a party to the proceeding. This clause will survive closing.
230   **(c) Mediation and Arbitration; Expenses:** "Mediation" is a process in which parties attempt to resolve a dispute by
231   submitting it to an impartial mediator who facilitates the resolution of the dispute but who is not empowered to impose a
232   settlement on the parties. Mediation will be in accordance with the rules of the American Mediation Association or other
233   mediator agreed on by the parties. The parties will equally divide the mediation fee, if any. "Arbitration" is a process in
234   which the parties resolve a dispute by a hearing before a neutral person who decides the matter and whose decision is
235   binding on the parties. Arbitration will be in accordance with the rules of the American Arbitration Association or other
236   arbitrator agreed on by the parties. Each party to any arbitration will pay its own fees, costs and expenses, including
237   attorney's fees, and will equally split the arbitrators' fees and administrative fees of arbitration.

238   **ESCROW AGENT AND BROKER**
239   **17. ESCROW AGENT:** Buyer and Seller authorize Escrow Agent to receive, deposit and hold funds and other items in escrow and,
240   subject to clearance, disburse them upon proper authorization and in accordance with the terms of this Contract, including
241   disbursing brokerage fees. The parties agree that Escrow Agent will not be liable to any person for misdelivery of escrowed items to
242   **Buyer** or **Seller**, unless the misdelivery is due to Escrow Agent's willful breach of this Contract or gross negligence. If Escrow Agent
243   interpleads the subject matter of the escrow, Escrow Agent will pay the filing fees and costs from the deposit and will recover
244   reasonable attorney's fees and costs to be paid from the escrowed funds or equivalent and charged and awarded as court costs in
245   favor of the prevailing party. All claims against Escrow Agent will be arbitrated, so long as Escrow Agent consents to arbitrate.

246*   **Buyer** (____)(____) and **Seller** (____)(____) acknowledge receipt of a copy of this page, which is Page 3 of 4 Pages.

FAR-5 Rev. 10/98 ©1998 Florida Association of Realtors® All Rights Reserved

This form is licensed for use with **Formulator**® Forms Software by ISG McAllister Publishing, Inc. 800-336-1027

247 **18. PROFESSIONAL ADVICE; BROKER LIABILITY**: Broker advises **Buyer** and **Seller** to verify all facts and representations that
248 are important to them and to consult an appropriate professional for legal advice (for example, interpreting contracts,
249 determining the effect of laws on the Property and transaction, status of title, foreign investor reporting requirements, etc.) and
250 for tax, property condition, environmental and other specialized advice. **Buyer** acknowledges that Broker does not reside in the
251 Property and that all representations (oral, written or otherwise) by Broker are based on **Seller** representations or public records
252 unless Broker indicates personal verification of the representation. **Buyer agrees to rely solely on Seller, professional inspectors**
253 **and governmental agencies for verification of the Property condition, square footage and facts that materially affect Property**
254 **value. Buyer** and **Seller** respectively will pay all costs and expenses, including reasonable attorneys' fees at all levels, incurred by
255 Broker and Broker's officers, directors, agents and employees in connection with or arising from **Buyer's** or **Seller's**
256 misstatement or failure to perform contractual obligations. **Buyer** and **Seller** hold harmless and release Broker and Broker's
257 officers, directors, agents and employees from all liability for loss or damage based on **(1) Buyer's** or **Seller's** misstatement or
258 failure to perform contractual obligations; **(2)** Broker's performance, at **Buyer's** and /or **Seller's** request, of any task beyond the
259 scope of services regulated by Chapter 475, F.S., as amended, including Broker's referral, recommendation or retention of any
260 vendor, **(3)** products or services provided by any vendor; and **(4)** expenses incurred by any vendor. **Buyer** and **Seller** each assume full
261 responsibility for selecting and compensating their respective vendors. This paragraph will not relieve Broker of statutory
262 obligations. For purposes of this paragraph, Broker will be treated as a party to this Contract. This paragraph will survive closing.

263 **19. BROKERS**: The licensee(s) and brokerage(s) named below are collectively referred to as "Broker". **Seller** and **Buyer**
264 acknowledge that the brokerage(s) named below are the procuring cause of this transaction. **Instruction to Closing Agent: Seller**
265 and **Buyer** direct closing agent to disburse at closing the full amount of the brokerage fees as specified in separate brokerage
266 agreements with the parties and cooperative agreements between the brokers, unless Broker has retained such fees from the
267 escrowed funds. In the absence of such brokerage agreements, closing agent will disburse brokerage fees as indicated below.
268* _____
269 *Real Estate Licensee*   *Real Estate Licensee*
270* _____
271* *Brokerage / Brokerage Fee:* _____   *Brokerage / Brokerage Fee:* _____

272   **ADDENDA AND ADDITIONAL TERMS**
273 **20. ADDENDA**: The following additional terms are included in addenda and incorporated into this Contract (check if applicable):
274* ☐ A. Condo. Assn.   ☐ G. New Mort. Rates   ☐ M. Housing Older Persons.   ☐ S. Sale of Buyer's Property
275* ☐ B. Homeowners Assn.   ☐ H. As Is w/Right to Inspect   ☐ N. Unimproved/Ag. Prop.   ☐ T. Rezoning
276* ☐ C. Seller Financing   ☐ I. Self-Inspections   ☐ O. Interest-Bearing Account   ☐ U. Assignment
277* ☐ D. Mort. Assumption   ☐ J. Insulation Disclosure   ☐ P. Back-up Contract.   ☐ V. Prop. Disclosure Stmt.
278* ☐ E. FHA Financing   ☐ K. Pre-1978 Housing Stmt. (LBP)   ☐ Q. Broker Pers. Int. in Prop.   ☐ Other _____
279* ☐ F. VA Financing   ☐ L. Flood Insurance Reqd.   ☐ R. Rentals   ☐ Other _____

280* **21. ADDITIONAL TERMS:**
281* _____
282* _____
283* _____
284* _____
285* _____
286* _____
287* _____
288* _____
289* _____

290   **This is intended to be a legally binding contract. If not fully understood, seek the advice of an attorney prior to signing.**

291   **OFFER AND ACCEPTANCE**
292* **(Check if applicable:** ☐ **Buyer** received a written real property disclosure statement from **Seller** before making this Offer.)
293 **Buyer** offers to purchase the Property on the above terms and conditions. Unless this Contract is signed by **Seller** and a copy
294* delivered to **Buyer** no later than _____ ☐ a.m. ☐ p.m on _____ , this offer will be revoked
295 and **Buyer's** deposit refunded subject to clearance of funds.

296* Date: _____   **Buyer:** _____   Tax ID/SSN: _____
297*   Print name: _____
298* Date: _____   **Buyer:** _____   Tax ID/SSN: _____
299*   Print name: _____
300* Phone: _____   Address: _____
301* Fax: _____
302* Date: _____   **Seller:** _____   Tax ID/SSN: _____
203*   Print name: _____
204* Date: _____   **Seller:** _____   Tax ID/SSN: _____
205*   Print name: _____
206* Phone: _____   Address: _____
207* Fax: _____
308* ☐ **Seller** counters **Buyer's** offer (to accept the counter offer, **Buyer** must sign or initial the counter offered terms and deliver a copy
309* of the acceptance to **Seller** by 5:00 p.m. on _____). ☐ **Seller** rejects **Buyer's** offer.

310*   **Effective Date:** _____   **(The date on which the last party signed or initialed acceptance of the final offer.)**

311* **Buyer** (____)(____) and **Seller** (____)(____) acknowledge receipt of a copy of this page, which is Page 4 of 4 Pages.

Appendix I
Settlement Statement

B. Type of Loan

	6. File Number	7. Loan Number	8. Mortgage Insurance Case Number
1. ☐ FHA 2. ☐ FmHA 3. ☐ Conv. Unis. 4. ☐ VA 5. ☐ Conv. Ins.			

C. NOTE: This form is furnished to give you a statement of actual settlement costs. Amounts paid to and by the settlement agent are shown. Items marked "(p.o.c.)" were paid outside the closing; they are shown here for informational purposes and are not included in the totals.

D. Name and Address of Borrower	E. Name and Address of Seller	F. Name and Address of Lender

G. Property Location	H. Settlement Agent	
	Place of Settlement	I. Settlement Date

J. Summary of Borrower's Transaction		K. Summary of Seller's Transaction	
100. Gross Amount Due From Borrower		**400. Gross Amount Due To Seller**	
101. Contract sales Price		401. Contract Sales price	
102. Personal property		402. Personal property	
103. Settlement charges to borrower (line 1400)		403.	
104.		404.	
105.		405.	
Adjustments for items paid by seller in advance		Adjustments for items paid by seller in advance	
106. City/town taxes to		406. City/town taxes to	
107. County taxes to		407. County taxes to	
108. Assessments to		408. Assessments to	
109.		409.	
110.		410.	
111.		411.	
112.		412.	
120. Gross Amount Due From Borrower		**420. Gross Amount Due To Seller**	
200. Amounts Paid By Or in Behalf of Borrower		**500. Reductions in Amount Due To Seller**	
201. Deposit or earnest money		501. Excess deposit (see instructions)	
202. Principal amount of new loan(s)		502. Settlement charges to seller (line 1400)	
203. Existing loan(s) taken subject to		503. Existing loan(s) taken subject to	
204.		504. Payoff of first mortgage loan	
205.		505. Payoff of second mortgage loan	
206.		506.	
207.		507.	
208.		508.	
209.		509.	
Adjustment for items unpaid by seller		Adjustments for items unpaid by seller	
210. City/town taxes to		510. City/town taxes to	
211. County taxes to		511. County taxes to	
212. Assessments to		512. Assessments to	
213.		513.	
214.		514.	
215.		515.	
216.		516.	
217.		517.	
218.		518.	
219.		519.	
220. Total Paid By/For Borrower		**520. Total Reduction Amount Due Seller**	
300. Cash At Settlement From/To Borrower		**600. Cash At Settlement To/From Seller**	
301. Gross Amount due from borrower (line 120)		601. Gross amount due to seller (line 520)	
302. Less amounts paid by/for borrower (line 220)		602. Less reductions in amt. due seller (line 520)	
303. Cash ☐ From ☐ To Borrower		**603. Cash** ☐ To ☐ From Seller	

700. Total Sales/Broker's Commission based on price $ @ % =			Paid From Borrower's Funds at Settlement	Paid From Seller's Funds at Settlement
Division of Commission (line 700) as follows:				
701. $ to				
702. $ to				
703. Commission paid at Settlement				
704.				
800. Items Payable In Connection With Loan				
801. Loan Origination Fee %				
802. Loan Discount %				
803. Appraisal Fee to				
804. Credit Report to				
805. Lender's Inspection Fee				
806. Mortgage Insurance Application Fee to				
807. Assumption Fee				
808.				
809.				
810.				
811.				
900. Items Required By Lender To Be Paid in Advance				
901. Interest From to @ $ /day				
902. Mortgage Insurance Premium for months to				
903. Hazard Insurance Premium for years to				
904. years to				
905.				
1000. Reserves Deposited With Lender				
1001. Hazard insurance months @ $ per month				
1002. Mortgage insurance months @ $ per month				
1003. City property taxes months @ $ per month				
1004. County property taxes months @ $ per month				
1005. Annual assessments months @ $ per month				
1006. months @ $ per month				
1007. months @ $ per month				
1008. months @ $ per month				
1100. Title Charges				
1101. Settlement or closing fee to				
1102. Abstract or title search to				
1103. Title examination to				
1104. Title insurance binder to				
1105. Document preparation to				
1106. Notary fees to				
1107. Attorney's fees to				
(includes above items numbers:)				
1108. Title insurance to				
(includes above items numbers:)				
1109. Lender's coverage $				
1110. Owner's coverage $				
1111.				
1112.				
1113.				
1200. Government Recording and Transfer Charges				
1201. Recording fees: Deed $; Mortgage $; Release $				
1202. City/county tax/stamps: Deed $; Mortgage $				
1203. State tax/stamps: Deed $; Mortgage $				
1204.				
1205.				
1300. Additional Settlement Charges				
1301. Survey to				
1302. Pest inspection to				
1303.				
1304.				
1305.				

1400. Total Settlement Charges (enter on lines 103, Section J and 502, Section K)

Appendix J
Amortization Schedules

Mortgage Amount: $150,000.00   **Amortization Period:** 10 Years

Annual Interest Rate: 7.50%   **Annual Payments:** Monthly – 12

Number	Principal Payment	Interest Payment	Total Payment	Mortgage Balance
1	$843.03	$937.50	$1,780.53	$149,156.97
2	$848.30	$932.23	$1,780.53	$148,308.67
3	$853.60	$926.93	$1,780.53	$147,455.07
4	$858.94	$921.59	$1,780.53	$146,596.13
5	$864.30	$916.23	$1,780.53	$145,731.83
6	$869.71	$910.82	$1,780.53	$144,862.12
7	$875.14	$905.39	$1,780.53	$143,986.98
8	$880.61	$899.92	$1,780.53	$143,106.37
9	$886.12	$894.41	$1,780.53	$142,220.26
10	$891.65	$888.88	$1,780.53	$141,328.60
11	$897.23	$883.30	$1,780.53	$140,431.38
12	$902.83	$877.70	$1,780.53	$139,528.54
Year 1 Summary	**$10,471.46**	**$10,894.90**	**$21,366.36**	
13	$908.48	$872.05	$1,780.53	$138,620.07
14	$914.15	$866.38	$1,780.53	$137,705.91
15	$919.87	$860.66	$1,780.53	$136,786.05
16	$925.62	$854.91	$1,780.53	$135,860.43
17	$931.40	$849.13	$1,780.53	$134,929.03
18	$937.22	$843.31	$1,780.53	$133,991.80
19	$943.08	$837.45	$1,780.53	$133,048.72
20	$948.98	$831.55	$1,780.53	$132,099.75
21	$954.91	$825.62	$1,780.53	$131,144.84
22	$960.87	$819.66	$1,780.53	$130,183.97
23	$966.88	$813.65	$1,780.53	$129,217.09
24	$972.92	$807.61	$1,780.53	$128,244.16
Year 2 Summary	**$21,755.84**	**$20,976.88**	**$42,732.72**	
25	$979.00	$801.53	$1,780.53	$127,265.16
26	$985.12	$795.41	$1,780.53	$126,280.04

Mortgage Amount: $150,000.00 **Amortization Period:** 10 Years
Annual Interest Rate: 7.50% **Annual Payments:** Monthly – 12

Number	Principal Payment	Interest Payment	Total Payment	Mortgage Balance
27	$991.28	$789.25	$1,780.53	$125,288.76
28	$997.47	$783.06	$1,780.53	$124,291.29
29	$1,003.71	$776.82	$1,780.53	$123,287.58
30	$1,009.98	$770.55	$1,780.53	$122,277.59
31	$1,016.29	$764.24	$1,780.53	$121,261.30
32	$1,022.65	$757.88	$1,780.53	$120,238.65
33	$1,029.04	$751.49	$1,780.53	$119,209.62
34	$1,035.47	$745.06	$1,780.53	$118,174.15
35	$1,041.94	$738.59	$1,780.53	$117,132.21
36	$1,048.45	$732.08	$1,780.53	$116,083.75
Year 3 Summary	**$33,916.25**	**$30,182.83**	**$64,099.08**	
37	$1,055.01	$725.52	$1,780.53	$115,028.75
38	$1,061.60	$718.93	$1,780.53	$113,967.15
39	$1,068.23	$712.30	$1,780.53	$112,898.91
40	$1,074.91	$705.62	$1,780.53	$111,824.00
41	$1,081.63	$698.90	$1,780.53	$110,742.37
42	$1,088.39	$692.14	$1,780.53	$109,653.98
43	$1,095.19	$685.34	$1,780.53	$108,558.79
44	$1,102.04	$678.49	$1,780.53	$107,456.76
45	$1,108.92	$671.61	$1,780.53	$106,347.83
46	$1,115.86	$664.67	$1,780.53	$105,231.98
47	$1,122.83	$657.70	$1,780.53	$104,109.15
48	$1,129.85	$650.68	$1,780.53	$102,979.30
Year 4 Summary	**$47,020.70**	**$38,444.74**	**$85,465.44**	
49	$1,136.91	$643.62	$1,780.53	$101,842.39
50	$1,144.01	$636.52	$1,780.53	$100,698.38
51	$1,151.16	$629.37	$1,780.53	$99,547.21
52	$1,158.36	$622.17	$1,780.53	$98,388.85
53	$1,165.60	$614.93	$1,780.53	$97,223.26
54	$1,172.88	$607.65	$1,780.53	$96,050.37
55	$1,180.21	$600.32	$1,780.53	$94,870.16
56	$1,187.59	$592.94	$1,780.53	$93,682.57

Appendix J

Mortgage Amount: $150,000.00   *Amortization Period:* 10 Years

Annual Interest Rate: 7.50%   *Annual Payments:* Monthly – 12

Number	Principal Payment	Interest Payment	Total Payment	Mortgage Balance
57	$1,195.01	$585.52	$1,780.53	$92,487.56
58	$1,202.48	$578.05	$1,780.53	$91,285.07
59	$1,210.00	$570.53	$1,780.53	$90,075.08
60	$1,217.56	$562.97	$1,780.53	$88,857.52
Year 5 Summary	**$61,142.48**	**$45,689.32**	**$106,831.80**	
61	$1,225.17	$555.36	$1,780.53	$87,632.35
62	$1,232.83	$547.70	$1,780.53	$86,399.52
63	$1,240.53	$540.00	$1,780.53	$85,158.99
64	$1,248.28	$532.25	$1,780.53	$83,910.71
65	$1,256.09	$524.44	$1,780.53	$82,654.62
66	$1,263.94	$516.59	$1,780.53	$81,390.68
67	$1,271.84	$508.69	$1,780.53	$80,118.84
68	$1,279.79	$500.74	$1,780.53	$78,839.06
69	$1,287.78	$492.75	$1,780.53	$77,551.27
70	$1,295.83	$484.70	$1,780.53	$76,255.44
71	$1,303.93	$476.60	$1,780.53	$74,951.51
72	$1,312.08	$468.45	$1,780.53	$73,639.43
Year 6 Summary	**$76,360.57**	**$51,837.59**	**$128,198.16**	
73	$1,320.28	$460.25	$1,780.53	$72,319.15
74	$1,328.53	$452.00	$1,780.53	$70,990.61
75	$1,336.84	$443.69	$1,780.53	$69,653.78
76	$1,345.19	$435.34	$1,780.53	$68,308.58
77	$1,353.60	$426.93	$1,780.53	$66,954.98
78	$1,362.06	$418.47	$1,780.53	$65,592.92
79	$1,370.57	$409.96	$1,780.53	$64,222.35
80	$1,379.14	$401.39	$1,780.53	$62,843.21
81	$1,387.76	$392.77	$1,780.53	$61,455.45
82	$1,396.43	$384.10	$1,780.53	$60,059.02
83	$1,405.16	$375.37	$1,780.53	$58,653.86
84	$1,413.94	$366.59	$1,780.53	$57,239.92
Year 7 Summary	**$92,760.08**	**$56,804.44**	**$149,564.52**	
85	$1,422.78	$357.75	$1,780.53	$55,817.14
86	$1,431.67	$348.86	$1,780.53	$54,385.47

Mortgage Amount: $150,000.00
Annual Interest Rate: 7.50%

Amortization Period: 10 Years
Annual Payments: Monthly – 12

Number	Principal Payment	Interest Payment	Total Payment	Mortgage Balance
87	$1,440.62	$339.91	$1,780.53	$52,944.85
88	$1,449.62	$330.91	$1,780.53	$51,495.23
89	$1,458.68	$321.85	$1,780.53	$50,036.55
90	$1,467.80	$312.73	$1,780.53	$48,568.75
91	$1,476.97	$303.56	$1,780.53	$47,091.77
92	$1,486.20	$294.33	$1,780.53	$45,605.57
93	$1,495.49	$285.04	$1,780.53	$44,110.08
94	$1,504.84	$275.69	$1,780.53	$42,605.24
95	$1,514.25	$266.28	$1,780.53	$41,090.99
96	$1,523.71	$256.82	$1,780.53	$39,567.28
Year 8 Summary	**$110,432.72**	**$60,498.16**	**$170,930.88**	
97	$1,533.23	$247.30	$1,780.53	$38,034.05
98	$1,542.82	$237.71	$1,780.53	$36,491.23
99	$1,552.46	$228.07	$1,780.53	$34,938.78
100	$1,562.16	$218.37	$1,780.53	$33,376.62
101	$1,571.92	$208.61	$1,780.53	$31,804.69
102	$1,581.75	$198.78	$1,780.53	$30,222.94
103	$1,591.63	$188.90	$1,780.53	$28,631.31
104	$1,601.58	$178.95	$1,780.53	$27,029.73
105	$1,611.59	$168.94	$1,780.53	$25,418.14
106	$1,621.66	$158.87	$1,780.53	$23,796.47
107	$1,631.80	$148.73	$1,780.53	$22,164.67
108	$1,642.00	$138.53	$1,780.53	$20,522.67
Year 9 Summary	**$129,477.33**	**$62,819.91**	**$192,297.24**	
109	$1,652.26	$128.27	$1,780.53	$18,870.41
110	$1,662.59	$117.94	$1,780.53	$17,207.82
111	$1,672.98	$107.55	$1,780.53	$15,534.85
112	$1,683.43	$97.10	$1,780.53	$13,851.41
113	$1,693.96	$86.57	$1,780.53	$12,157.45
114	$1,704.54	$75.99	$1,780.53	$10,452.91
115	$1,715.20	$65.33	$1,780.53	$8,737.71
116	$1,725.92	$54.61	$1,780.53	$7,011.80
117	$1,736.70	$43.83	$1,780.53	$5,275.09

Mortgage Amount: $150,000.00   **Amortization Period:** 10 Years

Annual Interest Rate: 7.50%   **Annual Payments:** Monthly – 12

Number	Principal Payment	Interest Payment	Total Payment	Mortgage Balance
118	$1,747.56	$32.97	$1,780.53	$3,527.54
119	$1,758.48	$22.05	$1,780.53	$1,769.06
120	$1,769.47	$11.06	$1,780.53	$-0.42
Year 10 Summary	**$150,000.42**	**$63,663.18**	**$213,663.60**	

Mortgage Amount: $150,000.00   *Amortization Period:* 15 Years

Annual Interest Rate: 7.50%   *Annual Payments:* Monthly – 12

Number	Principal Payment	Interest Payment	Total Payment	Mortgage Balance
1	$453.02	$937.50	$1,390.52	$149,546.98
2	$455.85	$934.67	$1,390.52	$149,091.13
3	$458.70	$931.82	$1,390.52	$148,632.43
4	$461.57	$928.95	$1,390.52	$148,170.86
5	$464.45	$926.07	$1,390.52	$147,706.41
6	$467.35	$923.17	$1,390.52	$147,239.05
7	$470.28	$920.24	$1,390.52	$146,768.78
8	$473.22	$917.30	$1,390.52	$146,295.56
9	$476.17	$914.35	$1,390.52	$145,819.39
10	$479.15	$911.37	$1,390.52	$145,340.24
11	$482.14	$908.38	$1,390.52	$144,858.10
12	$485.16	$905.36	$1,390.52	$144,372.94
Year 1 Summary	**$5,627.06**	**$11,059.18**	**$16,686.24**	
13	$488.19	$902.33	$1,390.52	$143,884.75
14	$491.24	$899.28	$1,390.52	$143,393.51
15	$494.31	$896.21	$1,390.52	$142,899.20
16	$497.40	$893.12	$1,390.52	$142,401.80
17	$500.51	$890.01	$1,390.52	$141,901.29
18	$503.64	$886.88	$1,390.52	$141,397.66
19	$506.78	$883.74	$1,390.52	$140,890.87
20	$509.95	$880.57	$1,390.52	$140,380.92
21	$513.14	$877.38	$1,390.52	$139,867.78
22	$516.35	$874.17	$1,390.52	$139,351.44
23	$519.57	$870.95	$1,390.52	$138,831.86
24	$522.82	$867.70	$1,390.52	$138,309.04
Year 2 Summary	**$11,690.96**	**$21,681.52**	**$33,372.48**	
25	$526.09	$864.43	$1,390.52	$137,782.95
26	$529.38	$861.14	$1,390.52	$137,253.58
27	$532.68	$857.84	$1,390.52	$136,720.89
28	$536.01	$854.51	$1,390.52	$136,184.88
29	$539.36	$851.16	$1,390.52	$135,645.51
30	$542.74	$847.78	$1,390.52	$135,102.78
31	$546.13	$844.39	$1,390.52	$134,556.65

Appendix J

Mortgage Amount: **$150,000.00**   *Amortization Period:* **15 Years**

Annual Interest Rate: **7.50%**   *Annual Payments:* **Monthly – 12**

Number	Principal Payment	Interest Payment	Total Payment	Mortgage Balance
32	$549.54	$840.98	$1,390.52	$134,007.11
33	$552.98	$837.54	$1,390.52	$133,454.13
34	$556.43	$834.09	$1,390.52	$132,897.70
35	$559.91	$830.61	$1,390.52	$132,337.79
36	$563.41	$827.11	$1,390.52	$131,774.39
Year 3 Summary	**$18,225.61**	**$31,833.11**	**$50,058.72**	
37	$566.93	$823.59	$1,390.52	$131,207.46
38	$570.47	$820.05	$1,390.52	$130,636.98
39	$574.04	$816.48	$1,390.52	$130,062.94
40	$577.63	$812.89	$1,390.52	$129,485.32
41	$581.24	$809.28	$1,390.52	$128,904.08
42	$584.87	$805.65	$1,390.52	$128,319.21
43	$588.52	$802.00	$1,390.52	$127,730.69
44	$592.20	$798.32	$1,390.52	$127,138.49
45	$595.90	$794.62	$1,390.52	$126,542.58
46	$599.63	$790.89	$1,390.52	$125,942.95
47	$603.38	$787.14	$1,390.52	$125,339.58
48	$607.15	$783.37	$1,390.52	$124,732.43
Year 4 Summary	**$25,267.57**	**$41,477.39**	**$66,744.96**	
49	$610.94	$779.58	$1,390.52	$124,121.49
50	$614.76	$775.76	$1,390.52	$123,506.73
51	$618.60	$771.92	$1,390.52	$122,888.12
52	$622.47	$768.05	$1,390.52	$122,265.66
53	$626.36	$764.16	$1,390.52	$121,639.30
54	$630.27	$760.25	$1,390.52	$121,009.02
55	$634.21	$756.31	$1,390.52	$120,374.81
56	$638.18	$752.34	$1,390.52	$119,736.63
57	$642.17	$748.35	$1,390.52	$119,094.47
58	$646.18	$744.34	$1,390.52	$118,448.29
59	$650.22	$740.30	$1,390.52	$117,798.07
60	$654.28	$736.24	$1,390.52	$117,143.79
Year 5 Summary	**$32,856.21**	**$50,574.99**	**$83,431.20**	
61	$658.37	$732.15	$1,390.52	$116,485.42

Mortgage Amount: $150,000.00   **Amortization Period:** 15 Years

Annual Interest Rate: 7.50%   **Annual Payments:** Monthly – 12

Number	Principal Payment	Interest Payment	Total Payment	Mortgage Balance
62	$662.49	$728.03	$1,390.52	$115,822.93
63	$666.63	$723.89	$1,390.52	$115,156.31
64	$670.79	$719.73	$1,390.52	$114,485.51
65	$674.98	$715.54	$1,390.52	$113,810.53
66	$679.20	$711.32	$1,390.52	$113,131.33
67	$683.45	$707.07	$1,390.52	$112,447.88
68	$687.72	$702.80	$1,390.52	$111,760.16
69	$692.02	$698.50	$1,390.52	$111,068.14
70	$696.34	$694.18	$1,390.52	$110,371.79
71	$700.70	$689.82	$1,390.52	$109,671.10
72	$705.07	$685.45	$1,390.52	$108,966.02
Year 6 Summary	**$41,033.98**	**$59,083.46**	**$100,117.44**	
73	$709.48	$681.04	$1,390.52	$108,256.54
74	$713.92	$676.60	$1,390.52	$107,542.63
75	$718.38	$672.14	$1,390.52	$106,824.25
76	$722.87	$667.65	$1,390.52	$106,101.38
77	$727.39	$663.13	$1,390.52	$105,374.00
78	$731.93	$658.59	$1,390.52	$104,642.06
79	$736.51	$654.01	$1,390.52	$103,905.56
80	$741.11	$649.41	$1,390.52	$103,164.45
81	$745.74	$644.78	$1,390.52	$102,418.71
82	$750.40	$640.12	$1,390.52	$101,668.30
83	$755.09	$635.43	$1,390.52	$100,913.21
84	$759.81	$630.71	$1,390.52	$100,153.40
Year 7 Summary	**$49,846.60**	**$66,957.08**	**$116,803.68**	
85	$764.56	$625.96	$1,390.52	$99,388.84
86	$769.34	$621.18	$1,390.52	$98,619.50
87	$774.15	$616.37	$1,390.52	$97,845.35
88	$778.99	$611.53	$1,390.52	$97,066.37
89	$783.85	$606.67	$1,390.52	$96,282.51
90	$788.75	$601.77	$1,390.52	$95,493.76
91	$793.68	$596.84	$1,390.52	$94,700.08
92	$798.64	$591.88	$1,390.52	$93,901.43

Mortgage Amount: $150,000.00   **Amortization Period: 15 Years**

Annual Interest Rate: 7.50%   **Annual Payments: Monthly – 12**

Number	Principal Payment	Interest Payment	Total Payment	Mortgage Balance
93	$803.64	$586.88	$1,390.52	$93,097.80
94	$808.66	$581.86	$1,390.52	$92,289.14
95	$813.71	$576.81	$1,390.52	$91,475.43
96	$818.80	$571.72	$1,390.52	$90,656.63
Year 8 Summary	$59,343.37	$74,146.55	$133,489.92	
97	$823.92	$566.60	$1,390.52	$89,832.71
98	$829.06	$561.46	$1,390.52	$89,003.65
99	$834.25	$556.27	$1,390.52	$88,169.40
100	$839.46	$551.06	$1,390.52	$87,329.94
101	$844.71	$545.81	$1,390.52	$86,485.24
102	$849.99	$540.53	$1,390.52	$85,635.25
103	$855.30	$535.22	$1,390.52	$84,779.95
104	$860.64	$529.88	$1,390.52	$83,919.31
105	$866.02	$524.50	$1,390.52	$83,053.28
106	$871.44	$519.08	$1,390.52	$82,181.85
107	$876.88	$513.64	$1,390.52	$81,304.96
108	$882.36	$508.16	$1,390.52	$80,422.60
Year 9 Summary	$69,577.40	$80,598.76	$150,176.16	
109	$887.88	$502.64	$1,390.52	$79,534.72
110	$893.43	$497.09	$1,390.52	$78,641.30
111	$899.01	$491.51	$1,390.52	$77,742.29
112	$904.63	$485.89	$1,390.52	$76,837.66
113	$910.28	$480.24	$1,390.52	$75,927.37
114	$915.97	$474.55	$1,390.52	$75,011.40
115	$921.70	$468.82	$1,390.52	$74,089.70
116	$927.46	$463.06	$1,390.52	$73,162.24
117	$933.25	$457.27	$1,390.52	$72,228.99
118	$939.09	$451.43	$1,390.52	$71,289.90
119	$944.96	$445.56	$1,390.52	$70,344.94
120	$950.86	$439.66	$1,390.52	$69,394.08
Year 10 Summary	$80,605.92	$86,256.48	$166,862.40	
121	$956.81	$433.71	$1,390.52	$68,437.28
122	$962.79	$427.73	$1,390.52	$67,474.49

Mortgage Amount: $150,000.00
Annual Interest Rate: 7.50%

Amortization Period: 15 Years
Annual Payments: Monthly – 12

Number	Principal Payment	Interest Payment	Total Payment	Mortgage Balance
123	$968.80	$421.72	$1,390.52	$66,505.69
124	$974.86	$415.66	$1,390.52	$65,530.83
125	$980.95	$409.57	$1,390.52	$64,549.88
126	$987.08	$403.44	$1,390.52	$63,562.79
127	$993.25	$397.27	$1,390.52	$62,569.54
128	$999.46	$391.06	$1,390.52	$61,570.08
129	$1,005.71	$384.81	$1,390.52	$60,564.38
130	$1,011.99	$378.53	$1,390.52	$59,552.39
131	$1,018.32	$372.20	$1,390.52	$58,534.07
132	$1,024.68	$365.84	$1,390.52	$57,509.39
Year 11 Summary	**$92,490.61**	**$91,058.03**	**$183,548.64**	
133	$1,031.09	$359.43	$1,390.52	$56,478.30
134	$1,037.53	$352.99	$1,390.52	$55,440.77
135	$1,044.01	$346.51	$1,390.52	$54,396.76
136	$1,050.54	$339.98	$1,390.52	$53,346.22
137	$1,057.10	$333.42	$1,390.52	$52,289.12
138	$1,063.71	$326.81	$1,390.52	$51,225.41
139	$1,070.36	$320.16	$1,390.52	$50,155.05
140	$1,077.05	$313.47	$1,390.52	$49,078.00
141	$1,083.78	$306.74	$1,390.52	$47,994.21
142	$1,090.55	$299.97	$1,390.52	$46,903.66
143	$1,097.37	$293.15	$1,390.52	$45,806.29
144	$1,104.23	$286.29	$1,390.52	$44,702.06
Year 12 Summary	**$105,297.94**	**$94,936.94**	**$200,234.88**	
145	$1,111.13	$279.39	$1,390.52	$43,590.93
146	$1,118.08	$272.44	$1,390.52	$42,472.85
147	$1,125.06	$265.46	$1,390.52	$41,347.79
148	$1,132.09	$258.43	$1,390.52	$40,215.69
149	$1,139.17	$251.35	$1,390.52	$39,076.52
150	$1,146.29	$244.23	$1,390.52	$37,930.23
151	$1,153.45	$237.07	$1,390.52	$36,776.78
152	$1,160.66	$229.86	$1,390.52	$35,616.12
153	$1,167.92	$222.60	$1,390.52	$34,448.20

Mortgage Amount: **$150,000.00**   *Amortization Period:* **15 Years**

Annual Interest Rate: **7.50%**   *Annual Payments:* **Monthly – 12**

Number	Principal Payment	Interest Payment	Total Payment	Mortgage Balance
154	$1,175.22	$215.30	$1,390.52	$33,272.98
155	$1,182.56	$207.96	$1,390.52	$32,090.42
156	$1,189.95	$200.57	$1,390.52	$30,900.46
Year 13 Summary	**$119,099.54**	**$97,821.58**	**$216,921.12**	
157	$1,197.39	$193.13	$1,390.52	$29,703.07
158	$1,204.87	$185.65	$1,390.52	$28,498.20
159	$1,212.40	$178.12	$1,390.52	$27,285.79
160	$1,219.98	$170.54	$1,390.52	$26,065.81
161	$1,227.61	$162.91	$1,390.52	$24,838.20
162	$1,235.28	$155.24	$1,390.52	$23,602.92
163	$1,243.00	$147.52	$1,390.52	$22,359.92
164	$1,250.77	$139.75	$1,390.52	$21,109.16
165	$1,258.59	$131.93	$1,390.52	$19,850.57
166	$1,266.45	$124.07	$1,390.52	$18,584.12
167	$1,274.37	$116.15	$1,390.52	$17,309.75
168	$1,282.33	$108.19	$1,390.52	$16,027.42
Year 14 Summary	**$133,972.58**	**$99,634.78**	**$233,607.36**	
169	$1,290.35	$100.17	$1,390.52	$14,737.07
170	$1,298.41	$92.11	$1,390.52	$13,438.66
171	$1,306.53	$83.99	$1,390.52	$12,132.13
172	$1,314.69	$75.83	$1,390.52	$10,817.44
173	$1,322.91	$67.61	$1,390.52	$9,494.53
174	$1,331.18	$59.34	$1,390.52	$8,163.35
175	$1,339.50	$51.02	$1,390.52	$6,823.85
176	$1,347.87	$42.65	$1,390.52	$5,475.98
177	$1,356.29	$34.23	$1,390.52	$4,119.69
178	$1,364.77	$25.75	$1,390.52	$2,754.92
179	$1,373.30	$17.22	$1,390.52	$1,381.62
180	$1,381.88	$8.64	$1,390.52	$-0.26
Year 15 Summary	**$150,000.26**	**$100,293.34**	**$250,293.60**	

Mortgage Amount: $150,000.00   *Amortization Period:* 30 Years

Annual Interest Rate: 7.50%   *Annual Payments:* Monthly – 12

Number	Principal Payment	Interest Payment	Total Payment	Mortgage Balance
1	$111.32	$937.50	$1,048.82	$149,888.68
2	$112.02	$936.80	$1,048.82	$149,776.66
3	$112.72	$936.10	$1,048.82	$149,663.95
4	$113.42	$935.40	$1,048.82	$149,550.53
5	$114.13	$934.69	$1,048.82	$149,436.40
6	$114.84	$933.98	$1,048.82	$149,321.56
7	$115.56	$933.26	$1,048.82	$149,206.00
8	$116.28	$932.54	$1,048.82	$149,089.71
9	$117.01	$931.81	$1,048.82	$148,972.70
10	$117.74	$931.08	$1,048.82	$148,854.96
11	$118.48	$930.34	$1,048.82	$148,736.49
12	$119.22	$929.60	$1,048.82	$148,617.27
Year 1 Summary	**$1,382.73**	**$11,203.11**	**$12,585.84**	
13	$119.96	$928.86	$1,048.82	$148,497.31
14	$120.71	$928.11	$1,048.82	$148,376.60
15	$121.47	$927.35	$1,048.82	$148,255.13
16	$122.23	$926.59	$1,048.82	$148,132.90
17	$122.99	$925.83	$1,048.82	$148,009.91
18	$123.76	$925.06	$1,048.82	$147,886.16
19	$124.53	$924.29	$1,048.82	$147,761.62
20	$125.31	$923.51	$1,048.82	$147,636.31
21	$126.09	$922.73	$1,048.82	$147,510.22
22	$126.88	$921.94	$1,048.82	$147,383.34
23	$127.67	$921.15	$1,048.82	$147,255.66
24	$128.47	$920.35	$1,048.82	$147,127.19
Year 2 Summary	**$2,872.81**	**$22,298.87**	**$25,171.68**	
25	$129.28	$919.54	$1,048.82	$146,997.92
26	$130.08	$918.74	$1,048.82	$146,867.83
27	$130.90	$917.92	$1,048.82	$146,736.94
28	$131.71	$917.11	$1,048.82	$146,605.22
29	$132.54	$916.28	$1,048.82	$146,472.69

Appendix J

Mortgage Amount: $150,000.00			**Amortization Period:** 30 Years	
Annual Interest Rate: 7.50%			**Annual Payments:** Monthly – 12	

Number	Principal Payment	Interest Payment	Total Payment	Mortgage Balance
30	$133.37	$915.45	$1,048.82	$146,339.32
31	$134.20	$914.62	$1,048.82	$146,205.12
32	$135.04	$913.78	$1,048.82	$146,070.08
33	$135.88	$912.94	$1,048.82	$145,934.20
34	$136.73	$912.09	$1,048.82	$145,797.47
35	$137.59	$911.23	$1,048.82	$145,659.88
36	$138.45	$910.37	$1,048.82	$145,521.44
Year 3 Summary	**$4,478.56**	**$33,278.96**	**$37,757.52**	
37	$139.31	$909.51	$1,048.82	$145,382.12
38	$140.18	$908.64	$1,048.82	$145,241.94
39	$141.06	$907.76	$1,048.82	$145,100.88
40	$141.94	$906.88	$1,048.82	$144,958.94
41	$142.83	$905.99	$1,048.82	$144,816.12
42	$143.72	$905.10	$1,048.82	$144,672.40
43	$144.62	$904.20	$1,048.82	$144,527.78
44	$145.52	$903.30	$1,048.82	$144,382.26
45	$146.43	$902.39	$1,048.82	$144,235.83
46	$147.35	$901.47	$1,048.82	$144,088.48
47	$148.27	$900.55	$1,048.82	$143,940.21
48	$149.19	$899.63	$1,048.82	$143,791.02
Year 4 Summary	**$6,208.98**	**$44,134.38**	**$50,343.36**	
49	$150.13	$898.69	$1,048.82	$143,640.89
50	$151.06	$897.76	$1,048.82	$143,489.83
51	$152.01	$896.81	$1,048.82	$143,337.82
52	$152.96	$895.86	$1,048.82	$143,184.86
53	$153.92	$894.90	$1,048.82	$143,030.94
54	$154.88	$893.94	$1,048.82	$142,876.06
55	$155.85	$892.97	$1,048.82	$142,720.22
56	$156.82	$892.00	$1,048.82	$142,563.40
57	$157.80	$891.02	$1,048.82	$142,405.60
58	$158.79	$890.03	$1,048.82	$142,246.82

Mortgage Amount: $150,000.00   *Amortization Period:* 30 Years

Annual Interest Rate: 7.50%   *Annual Payments:* Monthly – 12

Number	Principal Payment	Interest Payment	Total Payment	Mortgage Balance
59	$159.78	$889.04	$1,048.82	$142,087.04
60	$160.78	$888.04	$1,048.82	$141,926.26
Year 5 Summary	**$8,073.74**	**$54,855.46**	**$62,929.20**	
61	$161.78	$887.04	$1,048.82	$141,764.48
62	$162.79	$886.03	$1,048.82	$141,601.69
63	$163.81	$885.01	$1,048.82	$141,437.88
64	$164.83	$883.99	$1,048.82	$141,273.04
65	$165.86	$882.96	$1,048.82	$141,107.18
66	$166.90	$881.92	$1,048.82	$140,940.28
67	$167.94	$880.88	$1,048.82	$140,772.33
68	$168.99	$879.83	$1,048.82	$140,603.34
69	$170.05	$878.77	$1,048.82	$140,433.29
70	$171.11	$877.71	$1,048.82	$140,262.18
71	$172.18	$876.64	$1,048.82	$140,089.99
72	$173.26	$875.56	$1,048.82	$139,916.74
Year 6 Summary	**$10,083.26**	**$65,431.78**	**$75,515.04**	
73	$174.34	$874.48	$1,048.82	$139,742.40
74	$175.43	$873.39	$1,048.82	$139,566.96
75	$176.53	$872.29	$1,048.82	$139,390.44
76	$177.63	$871.19	$1,048.82	$139,212.81
77	$178.74	$870.08	$1,048.82	$139,034.07
78	$179.86	$868.96	$1,048.82	$138,854.21
79	$180.98	$867.84	$1,048.82	$138,673.23
80	$182.11	$866.71	$1,048.82	$138,491.11
81	$183.25	$865.57	$1,048.82	$138,307.86
82	$184.40	$864.42	$1,048.82	$138,123.46
83	$185.55	$863.27	$1,048.82	$137,937.92
84	$186.71	$862.11	$1,048.82	$137,751.21
Year 7 Summary	**$12,248.79**	**$75,852.09**	**$88,100.88**	
85	$187.88	$860.94	$1,048.82	$137,563.33

Appendix J

Mortgage Amount: $150,000.00   **Amortization Period:** 30 Years

Annual Interest Rate: 7.50%   **Annual Payments:** Monthly – 12

Number	Principal Payment	Interest Payment	Total Payment	Mortgage Balance
86	$189.05	$859.77	$1,048.82	$137,374.28
87	$190.23	$858.59	$1,048.82	$137,184.05
88	$191.42	$857.40	$1,048.82	$136,992.63
89	$192.62	$856.20	$1,048.82	$136,800.01
90	$193.82	$855.00	$1,048.82	$136,606.19
91	$195.03	$853.79	$1,048.82	$136,411.16
92	$196.25	$852.57	$1,048.82	$136,214.91
93	$197.48	$851.34	$1,048.82	$136,017.43
94	$198.71	$850.11	$1,048.82	$135,818.72
95	$199.95	$848.87	$1,048.82	$135,618.76
96	$201.20	$847.62	$1,048.82	$135,417.56
Year 8 Summary	**$14,582.44**	**$86,104.28**	**$100,686.72**	
97	$202.46	$846.36	$1,048.82	$135,215.10
98	$203.73	$845.09	$1,048.82	$135,011.37
99	$205.00	$843.82	$1,048.82	$134,806.37
100	$206.28	$842.54	$1,048.82	$134,600.09
101	$207.57	$841.25	$1,048.82	$134,392.52
102	$208.87	$839.95	$1,048.82	$134,183.65
103	$210.17	$838.65	$1,048.82	$133,973.48
104	$211.49	$837.33	$1,048.82	$133,761.99
105	$212.81	$836.01	$1,048.82	$133,549.18
106	$214.14	$834.68	$1,048.82	$133,335.04
107	$215.48	$833.34	$1,048.82	$133,119.57
108	$216.82	$832.00	$1,048.82	$132,902.74
Year 9 Summary	**$17,097.26**	**$96,175.30**	**$113,272.56**	
109	$218.18	$830.64	$1,048.82	$132,684.56
110	$219.54	$829.28	$1,048.82	$132,465.02
111	$220.91	$827.91	$1,048.82	$132,244.11
112	$222.30	$826.52	$1,048.82	$132,021.81
113	$223.68	$825.14	$1,048.82	$131,798.12
114	$225.08	$823.74	$1,048.82	$131,573.04

Mortgage Amount: $150,000.00   *Amortization Period:* 30 Years

Annual Interest Rate: 7.50%   *Annual Payments:* Monthly – 12

Number	Principal Payment	Interest Payment	Total Payment	Mortgage Balance
115	$226.49	$822.33	$1,048.82	$131,346.55
116	$227.91	$820.91	$1,048.82	$131,118.65
117	$229.33	$819.49	$1,048.82	$130,889.32
118	$230.76	$818.06	$1,048.82	$130,658.55
119	$232.21	$816.61	$1,048.82	$130,426.35
120	$233.66	$815.16	$1,048.82	$130,192.69
Year 10 Summary	**$19,807.31**	**$106,051.09**	**$125,858.40**	
121	$235.12	$813.70	$1,048.82	$129,957.58
122	$236.59	$812.23	$1,048.82	$129,720.99
123	$238.07	$810.75	$1,048.82	$129,482.92
124	$239.55	$809.27	$1,048.82	$129,243.37
125	$241.05	$807.77	$1,048.82	$129,002.32
126	$242.56	$806.26	$1,048.82	$128,759.76
127	$244.07	$804.75	$1,048.82	$128,515.69
128	$245.60	$803.22	$1,048.82	$128,270.09
129	$247.13	$801.69	$1,048.82	$128,022.96
130	$248.68	$800.14	$1,048.82	$127,774.28
131	$250.23	$798.59	$1,048.82	$127,524.05
132	$251.80	$797.02	$1,048.82	$127,272.25
Year 11 Summary	**$22,727.75**	**$115,716.49**	**$138,444.24**	
133	$253.37	$795.45	$1,048.82	$127,018.88
134	$254.95	$793.87	$1,048.82	$126,763.93
135	$256.55	$792.27	$1,048.82	$126,507.38
136	$258.15	$790.67	$1,048.82	$126,249.23
137	$259.76	$789.06	$1,048.82	$125,989.47
138	$261.39	$787.43	$1,048.82	$125,728.08
139	$263.02	$785.80	$1,048.82	$125,465.06
140	$264.66	$784.16	$1,048.82	$125,200.39
141	$266.32	$782.50	$1,048.82	$124,934.08
142	$267.98	$780.84	$1,048.82	$124,666.09
143	$269.66	$779.16	$1,048.82	$124,396.43

Mortgage Amount: $150,000.00   **Amortization Period:** 30 Years

Annual Interest Rate: 7.50%   **Annual Payments:** Monthly – 12

Number	Principal Payment	Interest Payment	Total Payment	Mortgage Balance
144	$271.34	$777.48	$1,048.82	$124,125.09
Year 12 Summary	**$25,874.91**	**$125,155.17**	**$151,030.08**	
145	$273.04	$775.78	$1,048.82	$123,852.05
146	$274.75	$774.07	$1,048.82	$123,577.30
147	$276.46	$772.36	$1,048.82	$123,300.84
148	$278.19	$770.63	$1,048.82	$123,022.65
149	$279.93	$768.89	$1,048.82	$122,742.72
150	$281.68	$767.14	$1,048.82	$122,461.04
151	$283.44	$765.38	$1,048.82	$122,177.60
152	$285.21	$763.61	$1,048.82	$121,892.39
153	$286.99	$761.83	$1,048.82	$121,605.39
154	$288.79	$760.03	$1,048.82	$121,316.61
155	$290.59	$758.23	$1,048.82	$121,026.01
156	$292.41	$756.41	$1,048.82	$120,733.60
Year 13 Summary	**$29,266.40**	**$134,349.52**	**$163,615.92**	
157	$294.24	$754.58	$1,048.82	$120,439.37
158	$296.08	$752.74	$1,048.82	$120,143.29
159	$297.93	$750.89	$1,048.82	$119,845.36
160	$299.79	$749.03	$1,048.82	$119,545.58
161	$301.66	$747.16	$1,048.82	$119,243.91
162	$303.55	$745.27	$1,048.82	$118,940.37
163	$305.44	$743.38	$1,048.82	$118,634.92
164	$307.35	$741.47	$1,048.82	$118,327.57
165	$309.27	$739.55	$1,048.82	$118,018.29
166	$311.21	$737.61	$1,048.82	$117,707.09
167	$313.15	$735.67	$1,048.82	$117,393.93
168	$315.11	$733.71	$1,048.82	$117,078.82
Year 14 Summary	**$32,921.18**	**$143,280.58**	**$176,201.76**	
169	$317.08	$731.74	$1,048.82	$116,761.75
170	$319.06	$729.76	$1,048.82	$116,442.68

Mortgage Amount: $150,000.00   *Amortization Period:* 30 Years

Annual Interest Rate: 7.50%   *Annual Payments:* Monthly – 12

Number	Principal Payment	Interest Payment	Total Payment	Mortgage Balance
171	$321.06	$727.76	$1,048.82	$116,121.63
172	$323.06	$725.76	$1,048.82	$115,798.57
173	$325.08	$723.74	$1,048.82	$115,473.49
174	$327.11	$721.71	$1,048.82	$115,146.37
175	$329.16	$719.66	$1,048.82	$114,817.22
176	$331.21	$717.61	$1,048.82	$114,486.00
177	$333.28	$715.54	$1,048.82	$114,152.72
178	$335.37	$713.45	$1,048.82	$113,817.35
179	$337.46	$711.36	$1,048.82	$113,479.89
180	$339.57	$709.25	$1,048.82	$113,140.32
Year 15 Summary	**$36,859.68**	**$151,927.92**	**$188,787.60**	
181	$341.70	$707.12	$1,048.82	$112,798.62
182	$343.83	$704.99	$1,048.82	$112,454.79
183	$345.98	$702.84	$1,048.82	$112,108.81
184	$348.14	$700.68	$1,048.82	$111,760.67
185	$350.32	$698.50	$1,048.82	$111,410.35
186	$352.51	$696.31	$1,048.82	$111,057.84
187	$354.71	$694.11	$1,048.82	$110,703.13
188	$356.93	$691.89	$1,048.82	$110,346.20
189	$359.16	$689.66	$1,048.82	$109,987.05
190	$361.40	$687.42	$1,048.82	$109,625.64
191	$363.66	$685.16	$1,048.82	$109,261.98
192	$365.93	$682.89	$1,048.82	$108,896.05
Year 16 Summary	**$41,103.95**	**$160,269.49**	**$201,373.44**	
193	$368.22	$680.60	$1,048.82	$108,527.82
194	$370.52	$678.30	$1,048.82	$108,157.30
195	$372.84	$675.98	$1,048.82	$107,784.46
196	$375.17	$673.65	$1,048.82	$107,409.29
197	$377.51	$671.31	$1,048.82	$107,031.78
198	$379.87	$668.95	$1,048.82	$106,651.91
199	$382.25	$666.57	$1,048.82	$106,269.66

Mortgage Amount: $150,000.00   **Amortization Period:** 30 Years

Annual Interest Rate: 7.50%   **Annual Payments:** Monthly – 12

Number	Principal Payment	Interest Payment	Total Payment	Mortgage Balance
200	$384.64	$664.18	$1,048.82	$105,885.02
201	$387.04	$661.78	$1,048.82	$105,497.98
202	$389.46	$659.36	$1,048.82	$105,108.52
203	$391.89	$656.93	$1,048.82	$104,716.63
204	$394.34	$654.48	$1,048.82	$104,322.28
Year 17 Summary	**$45,677.72**	**$168,281.56**	**$213,959.28**	
205	$396.81	$652.01	$1,048.82	$103,925.48
206	$399.29	$649.53	$1,048.82	$103,526.19
207	$401.78	$647.04	$1,048.82	$103,124.40
208	$404.29	$644.53	$1,048.82	$102,720.11
209	$406.82	$642.00	$1,048.82	$102,313.29
210	$409.36	$639.46	$1,048.82	$101,903.92
211	$411.92	$636.90	$1,048.82	$101,492.00
212	$414.50	$634.32	$1,048.82	$101,077.50
213	$417.09	$631.73	$1,048.82	$100,660.41
214	$419.69	$629.13	$1,048.82	$100,240.72
215	$422.32	$626.50	$1,048.82	$99,818.40
216	$424.96	$623.86	$1,048.82	$99,393.45
Year 18 Summary	**$50,606.55**	**$175,938.57**	**$226,545.12**	
217	$427.61	$621.21	$1,048.82	$98,965.83
218	$430.29	$618.53	$1,048.82	$98,535.55
219	$432.98	$615.84	$1,048.82	$98,102.57
220	$435.68	$613.14	$1,048.82	$97,666.89
221	$438.40	$610.42	$1,048.82	$97,228.48
222	$441.14	$607.68	$1,048.82	$96,787.34
223	$443.90	$604.92	$1,048.82	$96,343.44
224	$446.68	$602.14	$1,048.82	$95,896.76
225	$449.47	$599.35	$1,048.82	$95,447.30
226	$452.28	$596.54	$1,048.82	$94,995.02
227	$455.10	$593.72	$1,048.82	$94,539.91
228	$457.95	$590.87	$1,048.82	$94,081.97

Mortgage Amount: $150,000.00   *Amortization Period:* 30 Years

Annual Interest Rate: 7.50%   *Annual Payments:* Monthly – 12

Number	Principal Payment	Interest Payment	Total Payment	Mortgage Balance
Year 19 Summary	**$55,918.03**	**$183,212.93**	**$239,130.96**	
229	$460.81	$588.01	$1,048.82	$93,621.16
230	$463.69	$585.13	$1,048.82	$93,157.47
231	$466.59	$582.23	$1,048.82	$92,690.88
232	$469.50	$579.32	$1,048.82	$92,221.37
233	$472.44	$576.38	$1,048.82	$91,748.93
234	$475.39	$573.43	$1,048.82	$91,273.54
235	$478.36	$570.46	$1,048.82	$90,795.18
236	$481.35	$567.47	$1,048.82	$90,313.83
237	$484.36	$564.46	$1,048.82	$89,829.47
238	$487.39	$561.43	$1,048.82	$89,342.08
239	$490.43	$558.39	$1,048.82	$88,851.64
240	$493.50	$555.32	$1,048.82	$88,358.14
Year 20 Summary	**$61,641.86**	**$190,074.94**	**$251,716.80**	
241	$496.58	$552.24	$1,048.82	$87,861.56
242	$499.69	$549.13	$1,048.82	$87,361.87
243	$502.81	$546.01	$1,048.82	$86,859.06
244	$505.95	$542.87	$1,048.82	$86,353.11
245	$509.12	$539.70	$1,048.82	$85,843.99
246	$512.30	$536.52	$1,048.82	$85,331.69
247	$515.50	$533.32	$1,048.82	$84,816.19
248	$518.72	$530.10	$1,048.82	$84,297.47
249	$521.96	$526.86	$1,048.82	$83,775.51
250	$525.23	$523.59	$1,048.82	$83,250.28
251	$528.51	$520.31	$1,048.82	$82,721.77
252	$531.81	$517.01	$1,048.82	$82,189.96
Year 21 Summary	**$67,810.04**	**$196,492.60**	**$264,302.64**	
253	$535.14	$513.68	$1,048.82	$81,654.83
254	$538.48	$510.34	$1,048.82	$81,116.35
255	$541.85	$506.97	$1,048.82	$80,574.50

Appendix J

Mortgage Amount: $150,000.00   *Amortization Period:* 30 Years

Annual Interest Rate: 7.50%   *Annual Payments:* Monthly – 12

Number	Principal Payment	Interest Payment	Total Payment	Mortgage Balance
256	$545.23	$503.59	$1,048.82	$80,029.27
257	$548.64	$500.18	$1,048.82	$79,480.63
258	$552.07	$496.75	$1,048.82	$78,928.56
259	$555.52	$493.30	$1,048.82	$78,373.04
260	$558.99	$489.83	$1,048.82	$77,814.05
261	$562.49	$486.33	$1,048.82	$77,251.56
262	$566.00	$482.82	$1,048.82	$76,685.56
263	$569.54	$479.28	$1,048.82	$76,116.02
264	$573.10	$475.72	$1,048.82	$75,542.93
Year 22 Summary	**$74,457.07**	**$202,431.41**	**$276,888.48**	
265	$576.68	$472.14	$1,048.82	$74,966.25
266	$580.28	$468.54	$1,048.82	$74,385.96
267	$583.91	$464.91	$1,048.82	$73,802.05
268	$587.56	$461.26	$1,048.82	$73,214.49
269	$591.23	$457.59	$1,048.82	$72,623.26
270	$594.93	$453.89	$1,048.82	$72,028.33
271	$598.65	$450.17	$1,048.82	$71,429.69
272	$602.39	$446.43	$1,048.82	$70,827.30
273	$606.15	$442.67	$1,048.82	$70,221.15
274	$609.94	$438.88	$1,048.82	$69,611.21
275	$613.75	$435.07	$1,048.82	$68,997.45
276	$617.59	$431.23	$1,048.82	$68,379.86
Year 23 Summary	**$81,620.14**	**$207,854.18**	**$289,474.32**	
277	$621.45	$427.37	$1,048.82	$67,758.42
278	$625.33	$423.49	$1,048.82	$67,133.08
279	$629.24	$419.58	$1,048.82	$66,503.84
280	$633.17	$415.65	$1,048.82	$65,870.67
281	$637.13	$411.69	$1,048.82	$65,233.54
282	$641.11	$407.71	$1,048.82	$64,592.42
283	$645.12	$403.70	$1,048.82	$63,947.30
284	$649.15	$399.67	$1,048.82	$63,298.15

Mortgage Amount: $150,000.00

Annual Interest Rate: 7.50%

Amortization Period: 30 Years

Annual Payments: Monthly – 12

Number	Principal Payment	Interest Payment	Total Payment	Mortgage Balance
285	$653.21	$395.61	$1,048.82	$62,644.94
286	$657.29	$391.53	$1,048.82	$61,987.65
287	$661.40	$387.42	$1,048.82	$61,326.25
288	$665.53	$383.29	$1,048.82	$60,660.71
Year 24 Summary	**$89,339.29**	**$212,720.87**	**$302,060.16**	
289	$669.69	$379.13	$1,048.82	$59,991.02
290	$673.88	$374.94	$1,048.82	$59,317.14
291	$678.09	$370.73	$1,048.82	$58,639.05
292	$682.33	$366.49	$1,048.82	$57,956.72
293	$686.59	$362.23	$1,048.82	$57,270.13
294	$690.88	$357.94	$1,048.82	$56,579.24
295	$695.20	$353.62	$1,048.82	$55,884.04
296	$699.55	$349.27	$1,048.82	$55,184.49
297	$703.92	$344.90	$1,048.82	$54,480.57
298	$708.32	$340.50	$1,048.82	$53,772.25
299	$712.75	$336.07	$1,048.82	$53,059.50
300	$717.20	$331.62	$1,048.82	$52,342.30
Year 25 Summary	**$97,657.70**	**$216,988.30**	**$314,646.00**	
301	$721.68	$327.14	$1,048.82	$51,620.62
302	$726.19	$322.63	$1,048.82	$50,894.42
303	$730.73	$318.09	$1,048.82	$50,163.69
304	$735.30	$313.52	$1,048.82	$49,428.39
305	$739.90	$308.92	$1,048.82	$48,688.49
306	$744.52	$304.30	$1,048.82	$47,943.97
307	$749.17	$299.65	$1,048.82	$47,194.80
308	$753.86	$294.96	$1,048.82	$46,440.94
309	$758.57	$290.25	$1,048.82	$45,682.38
310	$763.31	$285.51	$1,048.82	$44,919.07
311	$768.08	$280.74	$1,048.82	$44,150.99
312	$772.88	$275.94	$1,048.82	$43,378.11

Appendix J

Mortgage Amount: $150,000.00   **Amortization Period:** 30 Years

Annual Interest Rate: 7.50%   **Annual Payments:** Monthly – 12

Number	Principal Payment	Interest Payment	Total Payment	Mortgage Balance
Year 26 Summary	**$106,621.89**	**$220,609.95**	**$327,231.84**	
313	$777.71	$271.11	$1,048.82	$42,600.40
314	$782.57	$266.25	$1,048.82	$41,817.83
315	$787.46	$261.36	$1,048.82	$41,030.37
316	$792.38	$256.44	$1,048.82	$40,237.98
317	$797.34	$251.48	$1,048.82	$39,440.65
318	$802.32	$246.50	$1,048.82	$38,638.33
319	$807.33	$241.49	$1,048.82	$37,830.99
320	$812.38	$236.44	$1,048.82	$37,018.61
321	$817.46	$231.36	$1,048.82	$36,201.16
322	$822.57	$226.25	$1,048.82	$35,378.59
323	$827.71	$221.11	$1,048.82	$34,550.88
324	$832.88	$215.94	$1,048.82	$33,718.00
Year 27 Summary	**$116,282.00**	**$223,535.68**	**$339,817.68**	
325	$838.09	$210.73	$1,048.82	$32,879.92
326	$843.32	$205.50	$1,048.82	$32,036.59
327	$848.59	$200.23	$1,048.82	$31,188.00
328	$853.90	$194.92	$1,048.82	$30,334.10
329	$859.24	$189.58	$1,048.82	$29,474.86
330	$864.61	$184.21	$1,048.82	$28,610.26
331	$870.01	$178.81	$1,048.82	$27,740.25
332	$875.45	$173.37	$1,048.82	$26,864.80
333	$880.92	$167.90	$1,048.82	$25,983.88
334	$886.42	$162.40	$1,048.82	$25,097.46
335	$891.96	$156.86	$1,048.82	$24,205.49
336	$897.54	$151.28	$1,048.82	$23,307.95
Year 28 Summary	**$126,692.05**	**$225,711.47**	**$352,403.52**	
337	$903.15	$145.67	$1,048.82	$22,404.80
338	$908.79	$140.03	$1,048.82	$21,496.01
339	$914.47	$134.35	$1,048.82	$20,581.54

Mortgage Amount: $150,000.00

Annual Interest Rate: 7.50%

Amortization Period: 30 Years

Annual Payments: Monthly – 12

Number	Principal Payment	Interest Payment	Total Payment	Mortgage Balance
340	$920.19	$128.63	$1,048.82	$19,661.35
341	$925.94	$122.88	$1,048.82	$18,735.41
342	$931.73	$117.09	$1,048.82	$17,803.68
343	$937.55	$111.27	$1,048.82	$16,866.13
344	$943.41	$105.41	$1,048.82	$15,922.72
345	$949.31	$99.51	$1,048.82	$14,973.41
346	$955.24	$93.58	$1,048.82	$14,018.17
347	$961.21	$87.61	$1,048.82	$13,056.96
348	$967.22	$81.60	$1,048.82	$12,089.74
Year 29 Summary	**$137,910.26**	**$227.079.10**	**$364,989.36**	
349	$973.26	$75.56	$1,048.82	$11,116.48
350	$979.35	$69.47	$1,048.82	$10,137.14
351	$985.47	$63.35	$1,048.82	$9,151.67
352	$991.63	$57.19	$1,048.82	$8,160.04
353	$997.82	$51.00	$1,048.82	$7,162.22
354	$1,004.06	$44.76	$1,048.82	$6,158.16
355	$1,010.34	$38.48	$1,048.82	$5,147.82
356	$1,016.65	$32.17	$1,048.82	$4,131.17
357	$1,023.00	$25.82	$1,048.82	$3,108.17
358	$1,029.40	$19.42	$1,048.82	$2,078.77
359	$1,035.83	$12.99	$1,048.82	$1,042.94
360	$1,042.31	$6.51	$1,048.82	$0.63
Year 30 Summary	**$149,999.37**	**$227,575.83**	**$377,575.20**	

The Ultimate Residential Real Estate Glossary of Terms

Abstract of Title: A summary of the history of title to a property, made up of the original grant and all subsequent conveyances and encumbrances relating to the particular parcel of real estate.

Absorption Rate: The rate at which listed properties are sold or leased in a given market area.

Accredited Buyer Representative: This designation, offered by the Real Estate Buyer's Agent Council, is given to real estate agents who successfully complete coursework in buyer representation and close a minimum number of transactions.

Acre: An amount of land equal to 43,560 square feet.

Accessibility: The ease or convenience of reaching a site, considering its ingress and egress and proximity to support facilities and modes of transportation.

Ad Valorem: Literally means "according to value;" usually refers to a tax calculated by using a percentage of property value.

Adjusted Basis: See Cost Basis.

Adjustment Frequency Period: The amount of time between rate changes in an adjustable rate mortgage (ARM).

Adjustable Rate Mortgage (ARM): Variable rate loans that have indexes or margins that determine how and when the interest and payments amounts change.

Agency: A fiduciary relationship in which one person has the authority to represent another.

Agent: A person bound by certain fiduciary duties who has the authority to act on behalf of another in dealing with third parties in a real estate transaction. Also may be known as a Realtor, broker or single agent.

Agreement of Sale: See Contract for Deed.

Air Rights: The right to use the open space above real estate.

Amenities: Improvements to, or characteristics of, real estate that are marketable or valuable.

Amortization: The gradual paying down of a debt, such as a mortgage and note, by installment payments of the principal and accrued interest.

Annexation: The addition or assembling of one property to another.

Annual Percentage Rate (APR): The effective or actual interest rate representing total finance charges, including interest, loan fees, points and other charges, expressed as a percentage of the total amount of the loan. The Truth in Lending Act requires that the APR must be disclosed to the borrower within three business days of receiving a loan application.

Appraisal: A defendable, supportable estimate of the market value of real estate, as of a given date, for a specific purpose. See Market Value. Also called *Valuation*.

Appraiser: An expert that estimates the market value of real estate, usually for others, in a disinterested third-party capacity. An appraiser that is state-certified has completed a minimum number of reports and hours of appraisal coursework, appraised real estate for a minimum number of years and passed a state exam.

Appreciation: An increase in the market value of property caused by economic factors.

ARM: Adjustable Rate Mortgage.

ARM Rate Cap: The maximum amount an interest rate can increase at each periodic rate adjustment.

Assessed Value: The value of real estate for tax purposes as determined by a local taxing authority. This value may not represent, and is mostly lower than, market value.

Assessment: The charge against real estate as determined by a unit of government for taxation or levy, according to established rates, to pay for proportionate costs of improvements or services.

Asset: Real or personal property, encumbered or not, which has some value.

Assignment: The transfer of the right, title and interest in real property, mortgages, bonds, leases, or sales contracts, from one entity, known as the *assignor*, to another, known as the *assignee*.

Glossary

Assumable Mortgage: A mortgage that stays with the property once it is sold. An assumption is the financing of a real estate purchase where the buyer (borrower) takes over, or assumes, full personal responsibility and liability for payment of the existing mortgage and becomes a co-guarantor for payment of the mortgage note.

Balloon Payment: A mortgage payment associated with a balloon loan, usually greater than double the amount of the normal payment, which is due at the end of the loan term.

Basis: See Cost Basis.

Benchmark: A marker used by surveyors to locate various positions on land.

Beneficiary: The entity who is in receipt of property rights or other benefits, usually at the completion of the term of a trust agreement.

Binder Deposit: See Escrow.

Blanket Mortgage: A mortgage secured by pledging more than one property as collateral, or security, for the loan obligation.

Book Value: See Cost Basis.

Broker: A person who acts as an agent, bringing parties together to lease, buy or sell real estate, for a commission or fee.

Brownstone: An example of a townhouse-style residence that is usually owned in fee simple without mandatory fees or common areas.

Bundle of Rights: An owner's extent of control over real property.

Buyer's Market: A situation where the supply of a certain type of real estate exceeds the demand.

Capital Gain: The taxable profit derived from the sale, or increase in value, of an asset.

Capitalization: A method of real estate valuation, commonly used in the income approach, in which net income is divided by a desired capitalization rate of return to conclude the present market value of real estate.

Cash Flow: The net income from rental real estate or an investment. This is determined by subtracting all operating and interest expenses from the gross income. If income exceeds expenses, there is positive cash flow.

Caveat Emptor: Latin, meaning, "let the buyer beware"; buy at your own risk.

Certificate of Title: A document that is evidence of real estate ownership.

Chain of Title: A chronological list of documents, such as deeds, conveyances, mortgages, certificates of title or liens, that affect title to a specific piece of real estate.

Chattel: Tangible personal property. This can include mortgages or stocks, as well as cars, furniture, etc.

Chattel Mortgage: A mortgage secured by personal property.

Clear Title: A title that is unencumbered and free of limitations.

Client: Also known as the *principal*. This is the party that hires the real estate agent and whose interests are to be served by the words and deeds of the agent.

Closing: The end of a real estate transaction where money is exchanged, legal documents are signed and the seller gives title to a property to the buyer.

Cloud on Title (Cloud of Title): An encumbrance or claim that could have an adverse affect on a property's title if proven valid, but can also be proven invalid.

CMA: See Comparative Market Analysis

Collateral: Real or personal property pledged as security on a promise to repay a debt. This property would be forfeited to the lender if the borrower defaults on a loan.

Common Elements: Areas of a condominium, P.U.D., or cooperative that are owned, and used in common, by all owner/residents. All owners of such properties retain undivided interest in these common elements, or common areas.

Compound Interest: Interest paid on interest earned.

Computer Loan Origination Systems (CLO): A system that is provided by some real estate or mortgage brokerage offices to help sort through the various types of loans offered by different lenders.

Comparative Market Analysis (CMA): A report that real estate agents generate to determine the fair market value of a piece of property, based on recent comparable sales.

Condemnation: A process by which privately owned real estate is taken, without consent, for public use. This process is usually due to a judgment that a building is unfit for habitation, and is legal under the laws of eminent domain.

Conditional Contract: A contract stipulating that the title of a property remains with the seller until all conditions, qualifications or restrictions are met or fulfilled by the buyer.

Condominium: A shared ownership in real property where an individual unit or structure, usually delineated from interior wall to interior wall, is exclusively owned and undivided interest in all common areas is also retained.

Consideration: Something of value, such as a promise, money, or property, that is given in return for something of value as a part of a sales contract.

Construction Loan: A short term, open-ended mortgage used to finance the construction of a property.

Constructive Notice: Public notice usually offered in public records, legally sufficient to give inferred or implied notice, but not actual notice.

Contingency: A clause in a contract which provides that a certain act must be completed, or circumstance met, in order for the contract to be binding on both parties; a conditional element in a contract.

Contract for Deed: A contract stipulating that the purchase price is paid in installments, over a period of time during which the buyer has possession of the property, but the seller retains title until the terms of the contract are satisfied. This is usually an agreement between individuals, and is also known as a *land contract, installment contract* or *agreement of sale.*

Contribution, Principle of: A principle in real estate appraisal that states that any improvement to real estate of any kind is worth only what it adds to the property's market value, regardless of the improvement's actual cost.

Conventional Mortgage: A mortgage loan offered by an institutional lender or private party, made without any additional guarantees for repayment, such as FHA insurance, a VA guarantee or private mortgage insurance. Usually the loan is given at an 80 to 90 percent loan-to-value ratio, with real estate used as security.

Conversion: (1) A change to a different use, as in converting rental apartments into cooperative units; (2) A form of fraud, where there is an unauthorized confiscation of property that belongs to another.

Conveyance: A written document or instrument, such as a deed, mortgage or will, which transfers a property's legal title from one party to another.

Cooperative: A type of multi-unit residence where there is shared ownership similar to owning stock in a company. Each owner has joint liability for the mortgage, and possesses a proprietary lease through the purchase of shares in the corporation, partnership or trust that owns the building.

Cost: The actual price paid for a product or property.

Cost Approach: A technique of real estate appraisal that adds the replacement cost of improvements, less depreciation, to a property's land value in order to estimate its market value. This approach is more reliable and appropriate when appraising newer or atypical structures.

Cost Basis: Book value, or the original price paid for a property plus improvements, less depreciation, computed for income tax purposes.

Counteroffer: A new offer made in reply to a previous offer received that was not acceptable. This offer supercedes all prior offers.

Credit Union: A cooperative association in which members are usually paid higher interest rates on their savings accounts in comparison to other savings institutions. Members also can borrow money from a credit union, usually at lower interest rates than those charged by other lenders.

Curable: Economically feasible or cost efficient to fix. A depreciated item is curable if the cost necessary to fix the problem does not exceed the value that investment would add to a property.

Customer: Also known as the *prospect*. This is the party an agent works with to handle a real estate transaction, but is not the client (or principal).

Debt Service: The amount of money periodically owed as payments to amortize a loan.

Glossary

Deed: A written document that transfers the interest in real estate from one party to another.

Deed-of-Trust: See Trust Deed.

Deed Restrictions: Qualifications written into a deed that limit the use of real property.

Default: Failure to meet or perform a legal obligation, duty or promise when due.

Deferred Exchange: A trading of similar properties at a specified future time.

Deferred Maintenance: Necessary repairs or curable, physical deterioration that has not yet been corrected.

Deficiency Judgement: A judgment against a debtor for the difference between the amount owed and the amount received in a foreclosure.

Demand: The desire or need to buy goods or services; one of the four characteristics of value. See Value.

Density: The number of items per unit of area; usually pertaining to the ratio of people per square mile or dwelling units per acre.

Department of Housing and Urban Development (HUD): Active in residential programs like urban renewal, public housing, rehab loans and water and sewer grants, it is a federal department that regulates GNMA and FHA.

Department of Veteran Affairs (DVA or VA): The federal department that partially guarantees loans to veterans for the purchase or construction of a home.

Depreciation: A loss of value in real estate due to physical deterioration, functional problems, external forces or any other cause.

Diminishing Returns, Law of: The premise that additional expenditures beyond a certain point will not produce a return commensurate with the additional investment. The point at which additional upgrades to a home would be considered an overimprovement during renovation or construction is an example of this concept. See Overimprovement. Also known as the *Law of Decreasing Returns*.

Disintegration: A situation where values are declining in the life cycle of a property or neighborhood.

Documentary Stamp: A stamp issued as evidence of tax paid on a conveyance or deed. This tax is paid when the document is publicly recorded.

Dual Agency: A type of agency or relationship where a real estate agent fully represents both sides (seller and buyer) in a real estate transaction. This is not allowed in many states.

Duplex: A residential building consisting of two attached dwelling units.

Earnest Money Deposit: See Escrow.

Easement: A right or interest in the real property of another allowing the holder to some limited privilege, use or benefit. This conveys use, but not ownership, of a portion of an owner's property.

Easement by Necessity: An easement providing access to landlocked real estate.

Easement by Prescription: An easement acquired by use of another's land for a minimum number of years. This use is not specifically granted by the owner, but is understood.

Easement in Gross: An easement benefiting a person, but not attached to particular real estate and not transferred through conveyance of title.

Economic Life: The total length of time a property is expected to be useful, profitable, or yield a return on investment.

Efficiency Apartment: See Studio Apartment.

Effective Age: An age assigned to a building or a component of a building by an appraiser or building inspector that considers its condition, level of renovation and utility, rather than its actual age. Typically, estimated effective age will be subtracted from the estimated total economic life of a building to establish an estimated remaining economic life. See Economic Life.

Effective Demand: A circumstance in which a buyer not only has a desire to purchase goods or services, but has the financial means to do so.

Effective Rate: See Annual Percentage Rate.

Egress: The means of exiting from a property; an exit or outlet.

Eminent Domain: The right of government to assume ownership of private property for public use.

Encroachment: The illegal trespassing or placement of an improvement onto the property of another.

Encumbrance: An interest or right in real property that limits the title but does not prevent its conveyance by the owner.

Equilibrium: A situation where supply and demand is in balance and property values are stable.

Equitable Ownership: The right to use and enjoy real estate that is owned by another. For example, a mortgagor (borrower) has all the rights of ownership of a property, but has pledged the property to the mortgagee (lender) as security for the debt. Or, the beneficiary of a trust has an equitable interest in the trust property.

Equity: The value or interest an owner has in a property over and above any debt or lien against the property; the difference between a property's fair market value and the amount owed on the property.

Equity of Redemption: The right of a mortgagor (borrower) to redeem a property after forfeiture by paying the debt.

Escheat: The right of government to assume title or ownership of property when its owner dies without a will or heirs.

Escrow: The system by which money or other property is held by a disinterested third-party until the terms of the escrow instructions are fulfilled. Money deposited into an escrow account can be called an *escrow deposit*, a *binder deposit* or an *earnest money deposit*. In a typical residential real estate transaction, this amount is usually equal to one to five percent of the sales price.

Estate: The degree of interest, or rights, in real estate.

Estate at Will: The occupation and use of a property by a tenant for an indefinite period of time, which is terminable upon notice by either tenant or landlord.

Estate for Life: An estate that only exists during a specific person's lifetime.

Estate for Years: An estate that only exists for a specific, definite number of years.

Estate Tax: A tax on a deceased person's assets, estate or title to property upon transfer or conveyance to another.

Eviction: The legal dispossession of a borrower or tenant who is in breach of contract.

Examination of Title: The process of discovering possible liens or encumbrances upon title to property based on a title search or abstract.

Exchange: The trading of similar properties, usually done to avoid income tax.

Exclusive Agency Agreement: A contract that allows only one agent, or broker, to sell property, but the owner can also sell the property through his or her own efforts without paying a commission.

Exclusive Right to Sell: A contract that gives one listing agent, or broker, the right to a commission, regardless of who sells the property, including the owner.

Exclusive Buyer Representation: A specialty in real estate in which agents only represent the best interests of buyers, and do not act as dual agents or accept listings.

Execute: To validate, fulfill or complete. Usually, a real estate sales contract is executed when it is agreed to, signed and understood by both parties.

External Obsolescence: A type of depreciation, usually incurable, that is a result of adverse conditions outside a site. For example, street noise, pollution, negative economic forces, etc.

Fannie Mae: See Federal National Mortgage Association.

Feasibility Study: A study to determine the best use and design of a property or development, with information on projected expenses and income.

Fee Simple: The simplest, most absolute kind of ownership, in which an individual owns a property exclusively and title is unqualified or unencumbered. It is the best form of ownership because it conveys the highest bundle of rights.

Federal Home Loan Mortgage Corporation (FHLMC): A corporation providing a secondary market for mortgages issued by the members of the FHLB system. Also known as *Freddie Mac*.

Federal Housing Administration (FHA): A division of the Department of Housing and Urban Development whose main function is to insure private lenders that provide residential mortgage loans.

Federal National Mortgage Association (FNMA): A privately owned corporation created by Congress in 1938 to support the secondary mortgage market by purchasing and selling government under-written residential mortgages. Today, its stock is publicly traded. Also known as *Fannie Mae*.

FHA: See Federal Housing Administration.

Fiduciary: A position of trust between two parties in which one is responsible for protecting the best interests of the other.

Fiduciary Duties: The responsibilities a broker (agent) must obey by law. The duties are as follows: honesty, loyalty, confidentiality, full disclosure, accounting, skill, care and diligence. A broker must also present all offers in a timely manner.

First Mortgage: A mortgage that has lien priority over all other mortgages.

Fixed Expenses: Costs required to own real estate that are ongoing and unchanging through the year, such as real estate taxes and hazard insurance.

Fixed-Rate Mortgage: A mortgage in which the interest rate and monthly payments remain the same over the life of the loan.

Fixture: A item that was once personal property, but has been permanently affixed to land or improvements, thus converting it into real estate.

Foreclosure: A lender-initiated court action against a mortgage borrower who has defaulted on a loan, to enforce payment of the debt by selling the debtor's real estate.

Freddie Mac: See Federal Home Loan Mortgage Corp.

Free and Clear: Title to real estate that is unencumbered by mortgages or liens.

Freehold Estate: See Fee Simple.

Functional Obsolescence: Imperfections in the structure or design of a property that negatively affect marketability, functional utility or value. *Incurable Functional Obsolescence* is a situation where the money necessary to fix a property's problem exceeds the value that investment would add to a home.

Functional Utility: The ability of a property or building to be useful and functional, or the efficiency of a building's use in terms of style, design, floor plan, layout and sizes and types of rooms.

Ginnie Mae: See Government National Mortgage Association.

Government National Mortgage Association: A federal agency created in 1968 to assume special assistance government subsidized housing projects and liquidation functions of FNMA. It participates in the secondary market through its mortgage-backed securities pool.

Good Faith Estimate: According to the Real Estate Settlement Procedures Act (RESPA), lenders must provide this estimate of closing costs to borrowers no more than three days after the loan application is received.

Graduated Payment Mortgage (GPM): A mortgage that increases monthly payments at a certain rate over the length of the loan term.

Grantee: The person or party, buying, or receiving title to, a property.

Grantor: The person or party, selling, or giving title to, a property.

Gross Income: A property's total income before any expenses are deducted.

Highest and Best Use: A term used in real estate appraisal that describes the possible land use of a property that would produce its greatest income or value. That use may not necessarily be its present use, and must be physically possible, financially feasible and legally permissible.

Homestead Laws: Some states have laws that allow an individual to have his/her primary home, or homestead, protected from creditors. This means an individual is exempt from execution and forced sale of his/her home for debts. This does not include tax liens, vendors' liens, mechanics' liens or mortgage liens.

Homestead Exemption: Individuals who own a home and use it as their primary residence are entitled to a tax exemption of the assessed tax value.

HUD: See Department of Housing and Urban Development.

HUD-1 Settlement Statement: The form used at closing by the settlement agent to disclose to all parties of a real estate transaction their total closing costs.

Improvement: Any structure permanently affixed to land which adds to the value of real estate; any development of land or buildings.

Income Approach: A real estate appraisal technique used to valuate income-producing, or rental, properties by capitalization of its net income.

Ingress: A means of entering a property; an entrance.

Inheritability: The ability to leave real estate or property to heirs.

Interest: (1) A right, concern or share of something of value. (2) The premium, rent, or money paid for the use of borrowed money based on a certain rate.

Interim Loan: See Construction Loan

Investment: Money put towards an asset in expectation of income or profit.

Joint Tenancy: Type of ownership between more than one individual where, upon the death of an owner, the surviving owner(s) automatically take over that share. Also known as *Joint Tenancy with Rights of Survivorship*.

Land: Real estate without improvements.

Land Contract of Sale: See Contract for Deed.

Landlord: The owner of rented real estate; a lessor who leases or rents property to a tenant (lessee).

Layout: The floor plan of a building; the arrangement of walls, rooms, areas and partitions within a building.

Lease: A rental agreement or contract transferring the right to possession and use of an owner's real property to a tenant (lessee) for a specified period of time and for a specified rental payment.

Lease Option: A rental agreement allowing a lessee the right to buy the property if and when certain conditions are met. A small percentage of the rent payments may be credited toward the ultimate purchase price.

Leasehold: The property rights enjoyed by a tenant created by a lease.

Legal Nonconforming Use: See Nonconforming Use.

Lessee: Tenant.

Lessor: Landlord.

Leverage: The use of borrowed money to finance, or increase the returns on an investment

Liabilities: Debts or obligations that must be paid, or duties that must be performed.

Lien: A charge or claim against a property to secure a debt or obligation.

Linkage: The time and distance relationship between a specific property and a support facility. For example, the travel time and mileage between a home and a school.

Liquid Asset: An asset that can be disposed of promptly or easily converted into cash.

Listing: A written contract in which a broker is hired to sell or rent a property for an owner in exchange for a commission or compensation.

Littoral Rights: The rights, title or interests of property owners in and to the water, or the land under the water, abutting or adjacent to their property. This term is only associated with non-flowing water, like lakes or bays.

Living Trust: An arrangement transferring a property's title to a third-person (trustee), to be held during the lifetime of the owner (trustor).

Loan to Value (LTV): The ratio of the loan amount to the price or value of the property to be purchased.

Market Approach: See Sales Comparison Approach.

Market Value: The most likely sales price of real estate, as of a specified date, given a typically motivated and educated seller and buyer.

Millage Rate: A tax rate expressed in tenths of a cent. A tax rate of one mill per thousand means $1 of taxes per $1,000 of assessed value.

Mortgage: A pledge of real estate as security for the performance of an obligation or payment of a debt.

Mortgage Term: The amount of time in which a mortgage loan must be paid off.

Mortgagee: The lender.

Mortgagor: The borrower.

Multiple Listing Service: The service to which brokers belong that serves as an exchange of information as to what houses are for sale.

Neighborhood: An area defined by: (1) properties of similar land use, quality, or design; (2) natural or manmade boundaries, such as waterways, railroad tracks, highways, or buildings.

Net Income (Net Operating Income or NOI): See Cash Flow.

Net Worth: The value of an individual's assets less total liabilities (debts).

Nonconforming Use: A use that no longer conforms to current zoning, but is legally allowed due to a property's established and continuous use prior to the change to current zoning. It is sometimes referred to as a *Legal Nonconforming Use*, and is usually a result of an older property having been grandfathered into current zoning.

Note (Promissory Note): An executed instrument that is evidence of a promise to repay a debt at a specified time; an IOU.

Obsolescence: A loss of a property's value; a cause of depreciation. In an appraisal report, two forms of depreciation are functional and external obsolescence.

Opportunity Cost: The amount of equity, money or assets that could be earned by investing elsewhere.

Overimprovement: An improvement or upgrade that is relatively too costly or large and does not represent a profitable or cost-efficient investment, given the characteristics of the neighboring properties and the highest and best use of the land; investing more money in a structure than a person can recapture or recover.

Palladian: (1) Pertaining to the Italian style of architecture of Andrea Palladio; (2) a style of window with a round-headed archway, as depicted on the front cover of this book; (3) pertaining to wisdom, knowledge or study.

Personal Property: Property that is not permanently affixed to the ground; property that is not considered to be real estate.

PITI: Principal, Interest, Taxes and Insurance.

Planned Unit Development: A type of ownership in which an individual parcel of land and improvements are owned exclusively, but the property is subject to deed restrictions and the owner retains undivided interest in some common area. Side-yard setback requirements are usually eliminated and mixed land uses are allowed.

PMI: Private Mortgage Insurance.

Pre-approval: When a lender has fully investigated the borrower's ability to repay a loan based on various factors, and has actually set a limit on the amount that can be spent on a home. These factors ordinarily include a borrower's income, current obligations or debt, credit history and the amount of money the borrower is willing to put down for the purchase of a home.

Prepayment Penalty: Money the lender charges for paying off a loan before it is due.

Pre-qualification: An estimate a lender makes on how much they can lend a borrower. Usually, this is only a rough estimate based on factors that have not yet been verified, like a borrower's income, credit history and debt.

Principal: (1) The person, also known as the client, who hires an agent and whose interests are to be served by the words and deeds of the agent. (2) The amount of a debt or the balance due on a mortgage.

Principal, Interest, Taxes and Insurance (PITI): The typical components of a house payment. Lenders use these expenses in determining how much home a borrower can afford.

Private Mortgage Insurance (PMI): This is either an annual or monthly fee that may be required by the lender if a borrower puts less than 20 percent down on a home purchase. PMI serves to help protect lenders against the potential costs of foreclosure.

Progression: An appraisal concept that the value of an inferior property is enhanced by its close proximity to superior properties. This is closely associated with the economic *Theory of Conformity*, which states that property values tend to conform to the median price or value within a given market.

Promissory Note: See Note.

Proprietary Lease: A type of lease given to shareholders (owner/occupants) in a cooperative corporation.

Proration: The dividing of income or expenses proportionately according to relative time or amount of use. Also called *Pro Rata Share*.

Prospect: See Customer.

Quitclaim Deed: A written document that transfers the interest in property from one party to another, without warranties or obligations.

This is a common type of deed used with gift, probate, divorce or foreclosure transactions.

Real Estate: A portion of the earth's surface, extending downward to the center of the earth and upward into space, including all improvements permanently attached, erected or affixed to the land, and all legal rights therein.

Real Estate Investment Trust (REIT): An unincorporated trust, made up of at least 100 individuals, which invests in real estate. Title to property is managed and controlled by trustees.

Real Estate Owned (REO): Real estate owned by a lending institution, usually acquired through foreclosure.

Real Estate Settlement Procedures Act (RESPA): A federal law enacted in 1974 to give proper disclosure to borrowers regarding closing costs in a real estate transaction. Lenders are required to provide a special information booklet and a Good Faith Estimate within three business days of a receipt of a loan application. The settlement agent must also list all closing costs on a HUD-1 form, which must be provided to the borrower one business day before closing if requested by the borrower.

Real Property: Technically, this refers to the rights associated with real estate, but commonly it has the same meaning as real estate. See Real Estate.

Realty: See Real Estate.

Realtor: Someone who is associated with a broker that is a member of the National Association of Realtors. All Realtors are real estate agents, but not all real estate agents are Realtors.

Recognized Gain: Profit or gain from the sale or exchange of an investment that is currently subject to taxation.

Regression: An appraisal concept that the value of a superior property is adversely affected by its close proximity to inferior properties. This is closely associated with the economic *Theory of Conformity*, which states that property values tend to conform to the median price or value within a given market.

Regulation Z: The truth-in-lending part of the Consumer Credit Protection Act of 1968, requiring complete disclosure of all costs associated with most lending activity.

Replacement Cost: The cost of construction of a building that has similar utility to the building being appraised.

Reproduction Cost: The cost of construction of an exact duplicate of a building.

Return of Investment: The recovery of the amount invested, from income, reversion or the sale of an investment.

Return on Investment: The cash flow or net after-tax income derived from an investment divided by the cash invested, expressed as a percentage; the interest rate of return on capital.

Reversion: Cash or some benefit that an investor receives at the end of an investment.

Revitalization: A neighborhood life cycle characterized by renewal, renovation and increasing prices.

Right of First Refusal: A person's right to have the first opportunity to buy or lease real estate.

Riparian Rights: The rights, title or interests of property owners in and to the water, or the land under the water, abutting or adjacent to their property. Sometimes this term is used only in association with flowing bodies of water, like rivers or streams, but mostly it is used universally with any type of water.

Sales Comparison Approach: Most commonly used and most reliable approach to value for residential properties, which analyzes three or more recent sales similar to the property and makes adjustments to allow for property differences.

Scarcity: The limited supply of an item relative to the demand for it; one of the four characteristics of value. See Value. For example, there is a both a high demand and limited supply of waterfront real estate, so those properties will be marketable and more valuable in the future.

Section: 640 acres or one square mile of land.

Seller's Market: A situation where the demand of a certain type of real estate exceeds the supply.

Setback: A zoning rule or building code that requires a preservation of certain open areas surrounding a structure. A setback line delineates the area where building is prohibited beyond a prescribed distance from the edge of a structure.

Severalty Ownership: A type of ownership where a single owner has sole ownership of a piece of real estate, but the estate is inheritable.

Straight-line Depreciation: A way of calculating a building's depreciation that assumes a constant loss of value over a certain period of time.

Studio Apartment: A room that serves as a living room, dining area, bedroom and kitchen. Also called an *Efficiency Apartment.*

Sublease: A lease made between an original, primary tenant and another, new tenant. This lease is shorter than the original lease and does not relinquish the original tenant's liability.

Subordination Agreement: The act of allowing a new mortgage agreement to be placed in a superior position to an existing mortgage agreement.

Substitution, Principle of: The real estate appraisal concept that market value of a property is affected by the ability of a buyer to purchase substitute, comparable properties at a certain price. Estimating market value by analyzing the sales prices of comparable properties is the foundation of the market approach to value.

Superadequacy: A building component or structure having excess capacity or quality, as determined by market demand. An example would be a five-car garage in a small, two-bedroom home.

Supply: In real estate, the amount of similar properties available for sale or lease in a given market.

Supply and Demand: In real estate, the theory that states that the price of a property varies directly with demand, and inversely with supply.

Survey: The process by which a parcel of land is measured, its boundaries determined and a statement is made regarding the distances and quantity of the land. Flood zones and improvements to the land may also be described.

Survivorship, Rights of: See Joint Tenancy.

Tax Shelter: The ability of an investment to offer a tax advantages. For example, an owner of real estate can deduct mortgage interest and depreciation.

Tenancy by the Entirety: A special form of ownership for married couples where there are automatic survivorship rights.

Tenancy in Common: A type of ownership where multiple owners retain undivided interest in a property and have the right to leave his or her share to an estate or to chosen heirs.

Tenancy in Severalty: Ownership of property by one person only. Also called *Sole Tenancy.*

Time-share: A type of ownership in which ownership of one property is split between two or more parties. A separate agreement provides for the division of use of the property among the co-owners, usually for a fixed or variable time period.

Title: Proof of ownership.

Title Insurance: A guarantee or warranty by a title insurance company that there are no liens, defects or encumbrances that would prevent an owner from taking ownership of a property. Lender's title insurance protects the lender against losses resulting from title problems and owner's title insurance insures the owner's interest in the property.

Topography: The characteristics of the surface of land.

Townhouse: A single family, attached, two or three story dwelling unit. The term refers to a type of building design or architecture, not a type of ownership; a townhouse can be owned in fee simple or be a part of a planned unit development or a condominium. Also called a *Townhome.*

Transaction Broker: A type of agency practiced in some states in which an agent can represent both parties in only a limited form and serves only to facilitate the transaction. The agent handles all aspects of the transaction, but can't divulge any confidential information to either party.

Transferability: The ability to convey title or possession of goods; one of the four characteristics of value. See Value.

Triplex: A residential building consisting of three attached dwelling units.

Trust: An agreement in which property rights are held by a third-party for the benefit of another.

Trust Deed: A financing instrument in which the borrower/trustor conveys title into the hands of a third-party trustee to be held for the beneficiary/lender. When the loan is paid, title is given to the trustor. If default occurs, the trustee exercises the power of sale on behalf of the lender/beneficiary. Also known as a *Deed-of-Trust*.

Trustee: The third-party holding title in trust for the beneficiary and trustor.

Trustor: The originator of a trust; the one who is conveying title of a property to the trustee.

Truth in Lending Act (Consumer Protection Act): Also known as *Regulation Z*, this act obligates the lender to disclose to borrowers what their interest rate, points and mortgage broker fees will be. The lender must also detail any other payment information associated with the loan.

Undivided Interest: Fractional rights or interests in real property without physical division of the property into shares.

Utility: Usefulness or the ability of something to fill a need or provide a benefit; one of the four characteristics of value. See Value.

VA: See Department of Veteran Affairs.

Vacancy Rate: The percentage of square footage in a rental property or rental area that is vacant, not rented or unoccupied.

Valuation: An estimate of an asset's worth as of a given date; an appraisal.

Value: The monetary worth of something. The four characteristics of value are demand, utility, scarcity and transferability.

Variance: A legal permit or authorization of a use of a specific parcel that does not conform to the zoning of the rest of the immediate area.

Warranty Deed: A deed that conveys and guarantees good title, free and clear of all encumbrances, and the right of possession, with all exceptions detailed in the document.

Water Rights: See Riparian Rights or Littoral Rights.

Yield: Profit or income attributed to an investment.

Zoning: The regulations and ordinances set forth by local government that limit the use of real estate.

Index

185

Index

Index

Has this Book Been Helpful?
Why Not Order One For a Friend?

$19.95

Yes, I want to order _____copies of *The Smart Money Guide to Buying a Home*. Please send $23.25 for each book. (The price is $19.95 plus $2 for shipping and handling and $1.30 sales tax). This order must be accompanied by a check or a postal money order for the full amount. Allow 30 days for delivery.

Name _____

Company _____

Address _____

City_____ State _____ Zip _____

Send to: Palladian Publishing
            P.O. Box 320445
            Tampa, FL 33679